WOMEN IN CONGRESS

"What's a nice lady like you doing in this political game?" This question was asked in 1916 of Jeannette Rankin of Montana, the first congresswoman. The enigma continues even today, and freshman congresswomen will be asked the same question. Women hold only 5 percent of all elected offices in the United States. In recent years, they have begun to get the jobs they want at the salaries they deserve. Here are the stories of such prominent women in politics as Bella Abzug, Shirley Chisholm, and Millicent Fenwick, among others. You'll find these individuals are aspiring to a higher level of public service with a desire to take an active part in the governing of this country.

BOOKS BY ESSIE E. LEE

ALCOHOL—PROOF OF WHAT?
CAREERS IN THE HEALTH FIELD
MARRIAGE AND FAMILIES
WOMEN IN CONGRESS

Women
in Congress

ESSIE E. LEE

Photographs

JULIAN MESSNER
New York

Acc. 11/8/79

Designed by Miriam Temple

Manufactured in the United States of America

Library of Congress Cataloging in Publication Data

Lee, Essie E
   Women in Congress.

   Includes index.
   SUMMARY: Presents biographies of prominent women
in politics, including Bella Abzug, Shirley Chisholm, Millicent Fenwick, Elizabeth Holtzman, Barbara A. Mikulski,
and Cardiss Collins.
   1. Legislators—United States—Biography—Juvenile literature. 2. Women legislators—United States—Biography
—Juvenile literature. [1. Women legislators. 2. Legisla-
tors] I. Title.
JK1013.L43   328.73'092'2 [B] [920]   78-31947
ISBN 0-671-32896-4

Contents

Introduction

In recent years, women have begun to get the jobs they want at the salaries they deserve; they have gone into the courts to establish their rights in legal and social relationships; they have exercised new freedoms in life styles. But women have not yet made significant gains in the political life of the country.

Women hold only 5 percent of all elected offices in the United States. Only 13 percent of elected school board members are women; 9 percent of state legislators. In the 1976 national elections, the United States House of Representatives gained two new women members—but the total number dropped by one from the last session of Congress because three female incumbents did not seek re-election. Representatives Bella Abzug and Patsy Mink were unsuccessful in their bids for the United States Senate. Representative Leonor Sullivan retired after an exciting career that lasted almost twenty-five years. The Senate, often called "the most exclusive men's club in the world," has not had a female senator since Margaret Chase Smith retired in 1972.

How frequently we hear phrases like "she's as tough as nails" or "she thinks like a man." Such compliments aren't happily received by women who are merely exercising their talents. Such, however, has been the case for most women who wielded political influence and power down through the ages. Historical figures such as Elizabeth I, Catherine the Great, Isabella, Victoria, Golda Meir, and Indira Gandhi are remembered as world leaders rather than as women.

In 1972, Jean J. Kirkpatrick, a Georgetown University political science professor, studied the "who, why, and what" that influence female participation in politics. Several women's professional and business organizations nominated fifty-one experienced state senators and representatives to attend a three-day conference. The women came from twenty-six states. In small groups, they discussed how to make the transition from tenderfoot to sophisticated campaigner. In private, many revealed sacrifices, disappointments, and struggles experienced while achieving personal ambitions. Professor Kirkpatrick's study of women in American public life contains a description of the "political woman." Her characteristics include a desire to influence public events. She has the skills needed to exercise influence. The political female seeks and wields influence and has the desire to preserve that influence. Most of the women in the professor's study possessed these qualities.

"What's a nice lady like you doing in this political game?" The question was asked in 1916 of Jeannette Rankin of Montana, the first congresswoman. The enigma continues into 1977, and freshman Congresswomen Mary Rose Oakar and Barbara Mikulski will be queried in the same manner. For in the minds of too many, women who seek careers in politics are pushy, big-mouthed, and egocentric. They are power-driven, eccentric invaders into a male world. This image is changing, but not fast enough. Politically oriented women share the same desires, interests, and concerns of their non-political sisters. They are wives, mothers, and girl friends. They love their men, bear and nurture children, often wear designers' clothes as well as jeans, always practice good grooming, and even speak in dulcet tones. They do all of these and much more . . . because in order to make it, they have to be twice as good. No one ever lets you forget that you're a minority. So a congresswoman must balance an active political life with an equally demanding private life.

The political woman is not too different from other women

in our society. She just puts her desires and talents to work in a male-dominated arena and usually functions as effectively as her male colleagues. The Kirkpatrick study revealed some similarities between political women and male politicians. For example, most are born and reared in small towns, reside in the same place for many years, have the benefit of higher education with higher incomes and social status than their parents, and come from families which are active in community life.

There are psychological similarities too. Members of both sexes have strong egos, high self-esteem, a constant need for achievement, realistic expectations, a well-developed sense of maturity and security, and are practical in their thinking. Since careers in local and state politics do not require full-time participation, both men and women have time for other interests and activities. Continuing a law practice, operating a business, and maintaining a marriage and family can be easily managed by both. Most of the women studied felt that high offices such as speaker, majority leader and chairman of powerful committees would be barred to them. Tradition and convention dictate that these roles be given to men, and men are reluctant to share power.

Confronted with the statistics on how few women there are in positions of power, it is becoming more apparent to more and more women that until they do gain significant political power and influence, they will undoubtedly continue to suffer some forms of legal, economic, and social discrimination.

The congresswomen of the 94th and 95th Congresses never considered politics as men's business. As young girls, they were not deterred or hampered by the limitations of traditional female role behavior. They believed in themselves as individuals. This kind of identification runs through the lives of women who aspire to a higher level of public service.

Bella Abzug

Once upon a time, a girl born in the South Bronx section of New York City of immigrant Russian parents grew up to be elected to the House of Representatives and to run for the Senate of the United States. And she almost made it! This was just another of the long list of courageous acts by Ms. Bella Abzug, freedom fighter. She had more to lose than other senatorial candidates, yet she gave up her secure House seat to strike another blow for freedom. To Ms. Abzug, losing merely means a temporary setback. She began plans to seek the job of mayor of New York City. This has been described as the second most difficult job in the United States after the presidency, but that didn't stop her from throwing one of her famous hats "into the ring." She appeared on the ballot for the primary election held on September 8, 1977. Her opponents numbered seven . . . all men.

Bella, as she is affectionately called, became a fighter while attending Walton High School. President Franklin Delano Roosevelt and his New Deal programs greatly influenced this impressionable, energetic youngster. Bella listened to his plans for helping people and formulated some of her own. She would study hard and become a lawyer. A lawyer could effect change. Bella's natural precociousness and ability to

11

stimulate others to action were sharpened during the time she was class president at her high school and head of the student government at Hunter College. She was no closet idealist and spoke out against injustices at home and abroad. Bella had no way of knowing then that all the college debating and speechmaking were training for a very distant career, a career that would eventually take her to Washington and back.

Bella Savitzky had her heart set on Harvard Law School, but she settled for Columbia Law School. It was in New York, which would eliminate housing costs and reduce the need for travel expenses. At times, she could also eat at home. To meet tuition costs, Bella worked as a clerk, as a counter girl, and at an assortment of odd jobs. While involved with all these commitments, she also managed a courtship with Martin Abzug. He was a young man who was employed in a family business that manufactured blouses. The romance blossomed, although World War II separated them for a couple of years. On June 4, 1944, Bella Savitzky became Mrs. Martin Abzug. The next year, she earned a law degree. Martin Abzug turned his talents toward serious writing and the stock market, and Bella Abzug continued her fight for causes.

Some people call her brash, aggressive, loud, and talkative. She may be some or none of these things at various times. Basically, Bella Abzug's extraordinary energy and intelligence remind one of "La Pasionaria," that fervent woman who organized the Spanish Loyalists in their fight against Franco. Her drive, persistence, and passionate concern are as well known as her hats. "By the time I was eleven years old, I knew that I would study law. I believed law to be an instrument of social change, so I became active in the behalf of labor, civil rights, tenants, and consumers." Ms. Abzug is in her law office located in downtown Manhattan. The suite of rooms is cluttered with opened and unopened boxes and cartons.

Much of the material is part of her life as a former congress-woman. The walls are plastered with numerous awards and plaques recognizing her talents and contributions to New York and its citizens. There are others from national organizations too.

She continues in her usual pattern of rapid-fire speech. "I represented people against Senator McCarthy during the 'witch-hunt' period. I fought against systematic exclusion of Negroes from juries in the South during the early 1950s. My concern was general constitutional rights of all people. The explosion of nuclear bombs by the United States and the Soviet Union in 1960 disturbed me greatly. These events caused me to become more involved in world issues. This led to my playing a leadership role in the Women Strike for Peace movement."

The ringing of the telephone interrupts her for a moment. She gives precise instructions to her secretary and continues. "I tried to teach women who cared about nuclear testing some of the facts. This testing was creating fallout and strontium 90 in their children's milk! Women needed to become political. It wasn't enough for them to express feelings, they had to learn how to lobby, influence the political party system, and support candidates . . . but only when the candidates took a position they favored. They have to work against a candidate they can't support, too. So I then became an ally with people in the Democratic Party to help create better policies. We needed policies on the Vietnam War and policies that would open up the party process to women, minorities, and youth who had been left out of it."

Bella Abzug's activities as an activist are well known. Her entrance to Congress was by a route quite different from that of other congresswomen. She became known nationally initially through her work with various movements and her support of other candidates. "When people were interested in issues which would bring about change, I helped them. In this way, I helped many candidates get elected to Congress . . . people from all over the country. I led lobbies to Washington in behalf of Women Strike for Peace. I also played a major role in a Citizens' Test Ban Treaty campaign which helped to bring about the first partial nuclear test ban treaty signed by President John Kennedy." Ms. Abzug stops momentarily to reflect. "When I saw no change being made by the people I'd helped to elect . . . people were still being excluded because of their race, sex, or youth—the war continued—Nixon was beginning to close down the government and take it over—I finally allowed people to convince me to run for office." Her delivery is sharp and emphatic and her eyes narrow with indignation.

"I ran, the first time, in 1970, as an activist and a woman because I felt both roles were essential in the political process. My running was symbolic, since I represented the many women, youth, and minorities who were not benefiting from the democratic system. Our priorities were all wrong! We had a country that was not providing jobs, equality, decent programs in health, adequate housing, child care, and help for the elderly. Our tax balance was going for the wrong things. We were not discontinuing the arms race. Pollution was a growing problem. Our cities were deteriorating. It was time that someone who was an activist and a woman came into the political arena. And that was why I ran for Congress."

Ms. Abzug did go to Washington and her membership in Congress did make a difference. In six years in Congress, Bella Abzug emerged as a forceful and eloquent national spokeswoman for peace, full employment, job-producing public works programs, federalization of welfare, openness in government, equal rights, consumer and environmental protection, aid to the cities, programs for senior citizens, and aid to Israel.

More than an advocate, she was among the most productive members of the House, author of dozens of key and unprecedented bills, including the first equal credit law, the first bill providing federal aid to operate mass transportation, multi-million dollar economic development, and jobs programs, and the first law authorizing federal repayment to New York and other cities for the cost incurred protecting the United Nations and foreign diplomats. This legislation had been sought unsuccessfully by other members of Congress for twenty years. In total, Abzug-sponsored legislation brought $6 billion to the state of New York, while producing thousands of new jobs.

Congresswoman Abzug was the sole New York City and senior New York State member of the House Public Works Committee, where she wrote major job and transportation bills and served on the House Government Operations Committee. She chaired the Government Operations Subcommittee on Government Information and Individual Rights. The subcommittee was the scene of her hearing on covert and illegal activities of the CIA, FBI, and other federal agencies. As subcommittee chairperson, she was chief legislative guardian of the Freedom of Information and Privacy Acts, which she coauthored. Ms. Abzug investigated illegal government interception of private communications and U.S. collaboration with Arab countries in discriminating against American Jews. Later, she coauthored and served as House floor manager and member of the Conference Committee for the Chiles-Abzug Government-in-the-Sunshine Act, which would open the public business of the executive branch of government to the public and press for the first time.

Another law authored by Representative Abzug provides $12 million for cleanup and improvement of New York harbor, including the widening and deepening of key connecting channels and a major beach reclamation project along the Rockaways. Ms. Abzug obtained the doubling of federal transportation funding to New York State, under a measure she introduced allocating $20 million nationwide for special transit projects for the elderly and handicapped. Her intervention resulted in an additional $800,000 for New York. This brought the total grant up to $1.8 million to be divided among projects throughout the state.

In yet another area, Congresswoman Abzug authored, introduced, and organized a national citizens' lobby to support her Welfare Reform Bill. This bill would standardize at 75 percent the federal reimbursement for all states' welfare costs. The measure, which was also introduced in the Senate by Senator Jacob Javits, would bring $1.3 billion in new federal aid annually to New York State and would benefit forty-eight other states as well.

An outspoken opponent of the SST airplane, Congresswoman Abzug unearthed the Nixon-Kissinger letters to European leaders promising in advance favorable United States action on import of the Concorde airplane. She authored an amendment, passed by the House, that would prevent SST landings at New York's John F. Kennedy International Airport.

A leader of the women's rights movement, Representative Abzug was the author of many women's bills; she is a founder and former chairwoman of the National Women's Political Caucus and serves on its advisory board. She is a member of NOW (National Organization of Women). The congresswoman was a floor manager of the effort in the House to retain equal opportunity in education (Title IX) laws, as well as a leader in the fight for congressional approval of the Federal Equal Rights Amendment. A member of the president's National Commission on Observance of International Women's Year, she served as congressional advisor to the July, 1975 IWY International Conference in Mexico City. At the meetings, she fought against the anti-Zionist Declaration of Mexico and persuaded the United States delegation to vote against it. Another project was a bill extending social security benefits to homemakers.

Congresswoman Abzug was among the earliest opponents of the Vietnam War. She toured Indochina twice on official, fact-finding missions. She sponsored a bill calling for general and unconditional amnesty. She was the first to call for the impeachment of President Nixon, and she opposed confirmation of both Gerald Ford and Nelson Rockefeller for the office of vice–president. Later, she opposed the Ford pardon of Nixon, and introduced a Resolution of Inquiry which resulted in President Ford's appearing before the House Judiciary Committee. This was the first time an American president had testified before a congressional investigating committee.

She had a high rate of attendance in Congress and consistently received high ratings on her voting record from the League of Women Voters, the AFL-CIO, senior citizens, consumer and conservative groups, a nun's organization, and peace and women's groups. A profile issued by the Ralph Nader study project in the fall of 1972 described her as a "remarkable, serious and highly articulate member of the House" and among its foremost proponents of environmental protection. She was named a House whip in January, 1975.

In April 1976, her congressional colleagues voted Bella Abzug the third most influential member of the entire House of Representatives, ranked behind only the two top Democratic leaders—Speaker Carl Albert and Majority Leader Thomas "Tip" O'Neill. The results of the survey were published in *U.S. News and World Report*. In a separate category, 1400 key Americans rated the congresswoman fifth among ten American women "who stand out as national leaders."

The former congresswoman's advice to young people is to care. "You must care about people and what happens to them. You must care about future generations. I cared about what was going to happen in the future to my two daughters . . . the kind of world and society in which they would live." Her daughters are Eve Gail, now twenty-seven years old and a sculptress, and Isobel, a law student. "I didn't enter the political arena until I was fifty years old. I had three successful careers as a wife, a mother, and as a lawyer. I entered politics because I am an activist. Someone had to speak out against the many injustices in this country. As a congresswoman, I continued to be an activist, which is rare in Congress . . . I worked for change within and outside the system."

Ms. Abzug knows that women have strengths that can be mobilized into political force. "Women must be encouraged and helped to run for office on all levels of government. The National Women's Political Caucus is trying to do this. We must help each other. For example, I played a major role in getting Mary Ann Krupsak elected to lieutenant governor. I campaigned upstate for Midge Costanza. Our young people must become more active too. It saddens me to say that only one-third of young people under twenty-one vote. These are the ones for whom we fought so hard in Congress to lower the voting age."

The ringing telephone gets her attention. After a short conversation, she hangs up the receiver. "I entered this out of a sense of commitment. I never thought about going into public life. It was the farthest thing from my mind. I always pictured myself as the critic . . . the person who applied pressure from the outside. I thought I was too independent to be a politician. But movement in our legislatures rarely happens without outside pressure. Pressure can come from women and youth. It took ten years for Congress to act against the Vietnam War. And these two groups were basically responsible for the war's end."

She removes the wide-brimmed, Italian straw hat. "Young people are too concerned with preparing themselves for careers. They tend to cut themselves off from the 'real world.' And then they get all prepared and know little about what the real world is about. Young people's challenge is to perfect democracy and one of the ways of doing this is through political power!" She emphasizes this point by tapping on the desk.

"Political power is, at the moment, in the hands of a very elitist group of people. Special interest groups influence the political arena and the only way we can change that is through getting involved ourselves! I think that if more women were in politics, they'd change power rather than having power change them. Women have special insights that men don't have. As the creators of life, we have a special concern for peace. Women could spend the government's money more wisely and more intelligently. Youngsters should know that political power can make a great difference in their lives as well as in the lives of others."

Ms. Abzug turned down an offer made by President Carter to join his administration in Washington. But on March 3, 1977, she accepted the president's offer of an appointment to the National Commission on the Observance of International Women's Year. Ms. Abzug served as presiding officer of the commission, which prepared for a national fall conference in Houston (November 18–21). The conference, which followed fifty-six state and territorial meetings on the rights and responsibilities of women, prepared recommendations for President Carter and Congress on ending barriers to equality for women.

On June 2, 1977, Ms. Abzug announced her candidacy for mayor of New York City. "We need urban policy and we don't have one in New York City!" she exclaimed. In an impromptu motorcade, she toured Manhattan shaking hands, answering questions, and greeting people along the streets and avenues. Cab and truck drivers, hucksters, saleswomen, clerks, professionals, street cleaners, students, and homemakers called out to her in affection, "Give 'em hell, Bella," "We love you, Bella."

Ms. Abzug's reply to her supporters was given in a subdued voice. "The mayoralty is an enormous responsibility that I do not take lightly. As a candidate for mayor, I am not promising to turn New York around overnight or to perform miracles. But I do promise to fight like hell to make this city work again and live again for the wonderful people in it."

Bella is controversial. She hassles, leads, cajoles, and inspires. Her eighteen counterparts miss her on the Hill. Many of them speak warmly of her fearlessness and ability to get the job done. They recall the farewell luncheon in her honor. Her staff offered a poem recited by her press secretary, Mr. Harold Holzer. One verse went like this:

> With hat firmly planted she never recanted
> on the stump, on the floor, in committee;
> standing up for the weaker, standing up to
> the speaker, a symbol of people and city.

As I turn to leave, I have a final question about her hats. She laughs in a friendly manner. "When I was a young lawyer, I worked for a law firm that represented unions. And they would send me to represent clients at the mediation or labor boards. Everyone would be polite and we'd all sit down. And we'd wait and wait! Finally someone would question the delay and start to leave. And the men would say, 'We're waiting for the lawyer.' And I would say, 'I'm the lawyer!' So I had an identity crisis. And then I started wearing hats, because in those days all professional women wore hats and gloves. I soon stopped the gloves. But I gradually became fond of wearing hats and wore many different ones. Then in my first campaign for a congressional seat, my aides would say 'Come meet Bella Abzug.' And people would say 'Which one is she?' And the aides would answer, 'She's the one wearing the hat!' So everybody thought that it was a campaign gimmick, but actually it was just my love of hats."

As planned, Ms. Abzug threw one of her famous, large hats into the primary campaign which sought to nominate the Democratic candidate for mayor of New York City. Her six male opponents included the incumbent, Mayor Abe Beame, and Congressman Edward Koch. Up until the final weeks, Ms. Abzug was considered a tough opponent to beat. Earlier polls had shown heavy support from minority and some union groups. However, as her campaign manager said later, "The powerful people in this town didn't want Bella to be mayor." Bella thought she could save the city that means so much to her. Yet, her give-'em-hell image, which some believe to be her greatest asset, was also her greatest liability. She polarized the electorate. On primary night, September 8, 1977, Ms. Abzug captured 17 percent of the vote and finished fourth behind Ed Koch's 20 percent, Mario Cuomo's 19 percent, and Mayor Abe Beame's 18 percent.

"The establishment which runs New York was not in favor of my candidacy," Bella states in a matter of fact manner. "I mean the banks, the real estate interests, the financial control board, the unions, and some of the newspapers. They run the city instead of the people and this makes me sad." Her face reflects a dejected spirit. "I wanted to represent the people. The other candidates represent special interest groups. As the campaign neared a close, other incidents replaced the real issues, the blackout and looting, the question of the death penalty, and a shift to conservatism." Bella sighs wearily, and her tone of voice grows softer.

The issue of capital punishment particularly was an irritant. "Out of the blackout came a feeling of fear in the city. The candidates became scapegoats. Instead of developing new programs that combat crime through meaningful police reform procedures, criminal justice review, stronger court measures, rehabilitation of offenders, and efforts to relieve youth unemployment, the candidates began to stimulate a call for capital punishment—an issue in which a mayor has no power whatsoever! It was a false issue."

Her eyes close momentarily and a sense of concern is heard in her voice. "I opposed capital punishment as I have in the past—in principle and in fact. Studies show that where it has been instituted, crime was not reduced. But instead it often created an atmosphere of violence." She waits for the jangling telephone to cease. "And, of course, there were the power plays and club house political tactics employed by some of the candidates. I am one of the few candidates in New York City who enjoys the support of a broad coalition of ethnic and religious minority groups. But this time with candidates already representing ethnic and minority groups, possible support for me became diffused." But even in defeat, Bella stimulated women to become more interested and involved in politics and franchise.

With the loss in the 1976 Senate primary and a fourth place finish in the 1977 mayoral primary, many people believed that Bella would write her political obituary. But she insisted in furthering her career and attempted to return to Congress by gaining the seat left vacant by Mayor Koch's election. Her supporters included *The New York Times*, whose editorial of January 14, 1978, lauded her qualifications and formidable, distinguished career. However, there were difficulties in getting her name on the ballot, which was achieved only after a court battle. Her Republican opponent, S. William Green, won the close election by 1,100 votes. A recount did not change the margin. It appeared that many former supporters tired of her boisterous political style, feared that she was on a losing streak, or considered her victory a foregone conclusion. Even with the endorsement of President Carter, Mayor Koch, Governor Carey, and Senator Edward Kennedy, Bella could not overcome that handicap of two-time-loser image, divisive techniques of her own party members, character attacks by opponents, apathy of women and young voters, and desertion by potential supporters.

"Of course, the press didn't contradict accusations of my association with Gay Rights, Women's Lib, and Communists, which didn't help. It snowed on election day and only 78 percent of the people came to the polls. Many stayed home believing that I would win easily." A pause to catch her breath interrupts her rapid fire speech. "I felt that these accusations should have been challenged, but my press people didn't take them seriously. So in the end, we lost by a fluke."

Ms. Abzug appears more depressed than angry. "Unfortunately, we are in a period where people tend to believe everything seen on television. At this moment in history, strong, independent-minded people not under the influence of special interest groups have a hard time getting elected," she concludes. During her six years in Congress, Bella delighted supporters and outraged detractors with her blunt opinions against the war and in favor of women's rights. She was not above calling House colleagues cowards and hypocrites, and they were not above resenting it. But times have changed. Bella's type of hard-hitting, two-fisted approach is passé. As Mr. Green, the new congressman, observed, "the age of confrontation is dead."

Ms. Abzug does not see herself politically finished. "I may run again. I'll have to think it through," she says. "I care for people and want to help, but meanwhile I'll find other ways to do it." Her voice is barely above a whisper and soft with heart-felt sincerity.

One way was made possible by President Carter's appointment of Bella to the position of co-director of the National Advisory Committee for Women in June 1978. She will help mobilize women to act in support of ratification of ERA. The committee will implement the plan of action adopted at the 1977 Houston conference. It will advise the president, the Congress, and the public as to what steps should be taken to improve the condition of women. Another area of responsibility of the committee is to relate and carry out procedures associated with the United Nations International Decade of Women, which ends in 1985. Ms. Abzug is an extraordinary political personality and wherever she serves, she makes an impact. Her jaw is firm and her eyes a bit misty, but one gets the feeling that the champion is only resting and readying for new and greater battles. Viva la Bella!

Lindy Hale Boggs

Throughout the history of America, there have always been families which are politically oriented. Corrine Morrison Claiborne was born into such a family. One of her ancestors is W. C. C. Claiborne, whom Thomas Jefferson appointed the first American governor of the Louisiana Territory; a more contemporary relative was her cousin deLesseps "Chep" Morrison, the late mayor of New Orleans. Some of her earliest recollections include lively political discussions and a family commitment to civic and political institutions.

Lindy, as she is known, Claiborne graduated from Sophie Newcomb College of Tulane University in New Orleans. During her college years, she was women's editor of the student newspaper, the *Hullaballoo*. Her future husband, Hale Boggs, was the editor. After graduation, Miss Claiborne taught history and English in the public schools of St. James Parish, Louisiana.

When Lindy Claiborne married the young Hale Boggs, her sophisticated knowledge of Louisiana history and her active interest in civic affairs was a good match for Boggs' keen intelligence and ambition to serve in politics. Their early years were spent in grass roots political activity, including formation of the People's League, a New Orleans-based political reform movement in the late 1930s and early 1940s.

Mrs. Boggs' first political activity came in 1939, when she served as a precinct captain for the 5th Precinct, 12th Ward of New Orleans. This experience was followed by many years of volunteer service at all levels in many organizations.

Hale Boggs served as majority leader of the House of Representatives until October 1972, when his airplane disappeared over Alaska. Lindy Boggs was urged to run for the vacant seat by many Louisianians, including her late husband's closest friends.

When asked why she felt confident about taking her husband's place in Congress, Mrs. Boggs replies, "I took an active part in Hale's work, and my role included running his campaigns, meeting with constituents, making speeches in his behalf, working with other Democratic women and congressional wives, organizing meetings, remembering people's names, and shaking hands." She pauses briefly. "I was finance chairman, vice–president and president of the Woman's National Democratic Club; founding member and president of the Democratic Wives Forum, and public relations chairman, program chairman, and president of the nonpartisan Congressional Club. You name it, and I probably did it one time or another over our years together in politics.

"In addition to the nitty-gritty, political work that needed to be done in the district or here in Washington, I also kept well informed about issues and often played the 'devil's advocate' in discussing legislation and public policy with my husband. During the Johnson and Kennedy years, Hale's leadership responsibilities during Democratic administrations gave me a special opportunity to help out. In addition to serving as co-chairman for the 1961 and 1965 inaugural balls, I was active in many of Mrs. Johnson's projects, including her beautification program."

She stops to recall other incidents. "Because I felt a special responsibility for contributing to the city of Washington, I was a board member for 12 years at Family and Child Services, and at Goodwill Industries and the Florence Crittendon Home. I was a member of the Congressional Circle for Friendship Settlement House, in addition to chairing fund raising projects for the Salvation Army, Mental Health, and Travelers' Aid. This experience gave me a special knowledge of social, economic, educational, and cultural problems so that I felt competent to advise Hale on the 'Great Society' legislation. I became chairman of a volunteer committee to get the initial Head Start pre-schooler program organized too."

It is obvious that Lindy Boggs was not the usual congressman's wife. She was a very active partner who was more than qualified for the position of member of Congress. "Friends and political colleagues whom Hale and I had known and worked with for many years urged me to run for his seat." Then she adds, "My children encouraged me also."

Hale Boggs' seniority and leadership position in the House could never be replaced, but in a March 1973 special election, 81 percent of the voters of the 2nd District agreed that Lindy Boggs was the best candidate to represent their interests in the United States Congress. She has been equal to that task, and, in 1974, the voters overwhelmingly re-elected her.

Congresswoman Boggs has introduced many bills, but is modest about her achievements. "I was elected in March 1973 and have held office a relatively short time—only four years—so it is difficult to list my 'greatest achievement' as a congresswoman. However, I feel that I do a good job of representing the interests of my constituents in the 2nd District of Louisiana and I work hard to help them with their needs. I have been an active supporter of many good pieces of legislation and I believe am successful in my efforts to encourage reasonable compromise and conciliation in committee and on the floor of the House."

A member of the House Appropriations Committee since January 1977, Mrs. Boggs serves on the Subcommittee on Public Works and the Subcommittee on Housing and Urban Development and Independent Agencies. In addition to her committee duties, the congresswoman was appointed by the Speaker of the House, Thomas P. O'Neill, Jr., to serve on the Board of Regents of the Smithsonian Institution. She is also the majority member from the House on the board of the American Revolution Bicentennial Administration (ARBA).

During the bicentennial, Mrs. Boggs served as chairwoman of the Joint Committee on Bicentennial Arrangements which coordinated activities on Capitol Hill for the House and Senate in observance of the nation's 200th anniversary.

Throughout the 1976 presidential election year, the congresswoman served on the National Campaign Steering Committee, which functioned as a liaison between the Democratic National Committee and the Carter-Mondale campaign.

In July 1976, Lindy Boggs served as chairwoman of the Democratic National Convention in New York City, presiding over the most peaceful and dignified convention in recent Democratic history.

Significant legislation passed during the 94th Congress which was co-sponsored by Lindy Boggs includes the Local Public Works and Capital Development Act, designed to boost employment and assist localities in constructing needed public facilities. In the field of housing, she was a co-sponsor of the Energy Conservation in Building Act, which provides assistance for weatherizing homes for low income families. The congresswoman co-sponsored the 1975 Middle Income

Housing Act; that year also saw the passage of legislation containing Mrs. Boggs' bill to establish a National Center for the Prevention and Control of Rape. Representative Boggs has sponsored numerous measures in the fields of health, energy research, credit rights, and education. During her first term in the House, she co-sponsored such major laws as the Housing and Community Development Act of 1974 and the Right to Privacy Act.

Congresswoman Boggs' political and community activities include membership on the 1974 campaign committee of the Democratic National Committee. She served on the national board of the American Field Service, and she is an honorary member of the board of directors of the metropolitan chapter of the National Foundation/March of Dimes. Mrs. Boggs is a member of the board of advisors for CLOSE-UP, a non-partisan forum for the involvement of youth in government. She has been active on the boards of Family and Child Services, Goodwill Industries, and Friendship Settlement House on Capitol Hill. She was a volunteer leader of Operation Headstart, the Office of Economic Opportunity's national program for pre-school children, and has a continuing interest in this and other economic opportunity programs. As a mark of recognition of her community service, the British Broadcasting Company made a documentary film about Lindy Boggs in 1965 entitled, "Woman of Action."

Congresswoman Boggs is special. From such a broad base of experience, she brings unusual talents to the job. "My daily work with Hale in New Orleans and in Washington was a kind of job experience which no other member could have enjoyed. This experience has given me immeasurable benefits, including an understanding of how the Congress and the federal government work, as well as a personal relationship with Hale's colleagues in the Congress. From 1956 on, I held national responsibilities at the Democratic National

Committee in campaigning, organizing, fund raising, and policy-making. I worked personally with many Democratic members in their campaigns."

Mrs. Boggs speaks about the personal characteristics that women bring to the job. "Women are especially sensitive to the issues which hit close to home and affect their families, including economics, unemployment, education, nutrition policy, welfare reform, job training, health care, care of the aging, environmental concerns, and the like."

Some congresswomen have said that each of them sees the issues as an individual. Others have commented about the lack of unanimity. Mrs. Boggs says, "The eighteen congresswomen are a most diverse group, each one reflecting her constituents and their interests. Therefore, we sometimes disagree on issues affecting our districts. This year has seen the formation of a Congresswomen's Caucus, and I anticipate that we will be working together more often in a coordinated fashion."

In the future, more and more young women will be combining careers with marriage and motherhood. Mrs. Boggs agrees. "Yes—more women are doing it all the time. Of course, my own children were grown when I ran for Congress. However, my daughter, Barbara Boggs Sigmund, is a successful freeholder (county commissioner) in Mercer County, New Jersey. She lives in Princeton with her husband and three young sons. Of course, it is especially important to have the help of a supportive and encouraging husband and father."

The career preparation for a seat in Congress can be almost anything. Since members of Congress represent the public in general, the membership should reflect the natural composition of our country's citizens. One member remarked, "Most of the people in Congress are there from one group: white, middle-aged men—lawyers and businessmen. They really don't represent America. Congress needs more women, some trade unionists, city planners, younger people, and minority members."

Nevertheless, everyone agrees upon a good basic education in school and community service. Mrs. Boggs' advice to young people is this, "I would advise young women (or men) who are interested in a career in public service to study in school subjects such as economics, political science, history, sociology, psychology, journalism, and business administration—all of which help develop an appreciation for people in all their human endeavors. I also encourage young people to get involved in their communities by working with civic or political groups so that they can develop the kind of skills and personal friendships needed to be effective in the public sphere."

Congresswoman Boggs' history of such service includes campaigning for Hubert Humphrey in 1968, serving as co-chairman of the Johnson-Humphrey Inaugural Ball in 1965, and traveling throughout the United States during the Johnson Administration to address groups in behalf of the First Lady's beautification program.

During the 1950s Lindy Boggs distinguished herself as chairman of "Operation Crossroads," a station wagon caravan campaign for presidential candidate Adlai Stevenson and Democratic congressional candidates. During these years, she was an active member and president of the Women's National Democratic Club. She was also a founder-member and president of the Democratic Congressional Wives Forum.

Everyone speaks of the long hours and comprehensive and demanding work load of a congressional member. Yet, there are benefits.

The congresswoman explains. "Like any hard job, the role of congresswoman has its difficulties and frustrations. However, the rewards are more than compensating. I do wish, however, that I had more time in which to read and reflect. And I would also like to be able to spend more time with my three children and eight grandchildren."

In addition to Barbara, who is married to Paul Sigmund, professor of politics at Princeton University, there are two other children. "My son is Thomas Hale Boggs, Jr. He is an attorney in Washington and his wife is the former Barbara Denechaud of New Orleans and a partner in Wonderful Weddings and Washington Whirl-Around. My other daughter is Corrine (or Cokie), a CBS reporter who is the wife of Steven V. Roberts, Greece Bureau Chief for *The New York Times*." She smiles and there is pride in her voice. "I have eight wonderful grandchildren, too." It is evident that her long, busy, and active career has not prevented her from maintaining a happy family life.

There are other rewards. In 1976, Congresswoman Boggs received the first AMVETS National Auxiliary Humanitarian Award to be given annually by the AMVETS Auxiliary for humanitarian endeavors. The congresswoman was also honored as the recipient of the 1976 St. Mary's Dominican College Distinguished Service Medal, the highest award conferred by the New Orleans institution for contributions to educational, civic, cultural, and other philanthropic causes. She was named one of ten outstanding persons of 1976 by the New Orleans Institute for Human Understanding. Mrs. Boggs is a fellow of the Tulane University Council, which advises and supports the president's efforts to attract superior students and faculty and financial resources to Tulane University in New Orleans.

In 1975, Trinity College in Washington, D.C., conferred upon Mrs. Boggs an honorary Doctorate of Public Service. In 1974, the congresswoman received the Weiss Memorial Award from the National Conference of Christians and Jews and the Mother Gerard Philan Gold Medal given annually to an outstanding woman by Virginia's Marymount College.

The congresswoman's thoughts on ERA are these. "When ERA was first passed by the Congress, the proponents had the edge in terms of organization and enthusiasm. Since 1972, the forces opposed to ERA have had time to organize and make a political impact on state legislatures." Like the other congresswomen, Mrs. Boggs favors the legislation.

Most congresswomen plan to keep their House seats for as long as their constituents want them. Mrs. Boggs is no exception. She says, "Right now I plan to continue to serve the people of the 2nd District of Louisiana as their congressional representative."

Mrs. Boggs has a hobby and applies herself to it when she can. "In addition to reading and visiting with friends, my most recent and consuming hobby has been restoring and furnishing my home in the French Quarter in New Orleans. It is a beautiful, old, Spanish-style townhouse on Bourbon Street."

In closing the interview, the congresswoman is asked her feelings about the influence of power. She replied in these words. "Power may be a corrupting influence in that it produces unusual opportunities for personal gain to which most citizens do not have access. Power also provides unusual opportunities for doing good since it is a way to make real changes in our system. Particularly in recent years, there has been an emphasis on examining negative aspects of authority by appointment or election due to revelations of wrong doings. Having spent many years in public life with my husband and as an elected official myself, I feel confident in saying that the vast majority of public servants are just what that term implies—dedicated men and women whose main goal is to give the public the best service possible."

Yvonne Braithwaite Burke

At what point does one advance from purely voluntary, community interest group activity to active politician? For Congresswoman Burke, it was the effect of the civil rights movement. She had many heroes and heroines involved in the movement, and this hero worship gave direction to her career. Public service had always been an interest, and she believed that being female had its advantages. Mrs. Burke's mother had a professional career but also worked at home. "Somehow or other," the congresswoman remembers, "I had an idea in the back of my mind that I could combine my desire to render service and be a political activist, if I had a husband who could support me. Then I could work on cases without charging anyone." She laughs at the thought of her early naivete. "I really was idealistic. I thought that with a husband's support, I'd be free to solve all the problems."

A native of Los Angeles, Mrs. Burke graduated from Manual Arts High School, received a Bachelor of Arts degree in political science from the University of California at Los Angeles and Juris Doctor degree from the University of

Southern California School of Law. She holds honorary Doctor of Law degrees from Virginia State College and Atlanta University. Mrs. Burke was admitted to the California Bar in 1956, soon after she received her law degree. While attending the Law Center at USC, she was a member of the Moot Court for Appellate Argument and received several honorary campus awards.

After graduation, she practiced law for ten years. Her involvement in community and local issues continued to widen. She served as a deputy corporation commissioner, a hearing officer for the police commission and as an attorney on the McCone Commission staff, which acted as the Watts riots investigatory body. Her experiences in the latter assignment helped to convince her of the need for change. The traditional role system makes it difficult for a woman to begin a political life before middle age, makes it difficult for her to combine roles, and makes it almost impossible for her to develop the skills and acquire the experience needed for a political career. But Mrs. Burke was willing to defy tradition.

"Working on the McCone Commission, representing dissidents in the civil rights cases and evaluating the establishment's analysis of the situation really made me focus on the possibility of running for office. An opening in a district became available. But everyone said, 'a black could never be elected, because it was just 27 percent black.' So we made an analysis of our own."

The future congresswoman and her supporters used census materials and came up with different statistics, which indicated that a minority candidacy had viability. "The person who is now the president of the Los Angeles Police Commission was my campaign manager. We were not organized nor did we have the support of the organized political machinery. We just forged ahead. It wasn't easy but we raised the money and carried out a successful campaign. We sur-

prised everyone by winning with an overwhelming margin!"
Her very attractive face brightens with a wide smile which is
neither affected nor boastful. One has to believe that under
that beautiful facade beats the heart of a fighter.

From 1966 until her election to Congress, Mrs. Burke
represented the 63rd District in the California State Assembly.
During the 1971 and 1972 sessions, she chaired the Assembly
Committee on Urban Development and Housing and served
on the Health, Finance, and Insurance Committees. As a
member of the state legislature, her efforts led to the enact-
ment of laws that greatly benefited California's indigent children, health insurance consumers, residents of homes for the
elderly and orphaned, and victims of government urban re-
newal and expansion projects.

Prior to her election to the House of Representatives, Mrs.
Burke served as vice chairperson of the 1972 Democratic
National Convention in Miami Beach. There, in the absence
of party chairman, Lawrence O'Brien, she presided over the
longest and, perhaps, most volatile session in convention history. In the 1976 Democratic National Convention, Representative Burke served on the Drafting Subcommittee of the
Democratic Platform Committee and was very active in drafting the party's platform. She also chaired the Task Force on
Foreign and Defense Policy, which drafted the foreign policy
plank for the platform.

Mrs. Burke was not married at the time of her election, but
she has opinions about the duality of roles women play. She
has the distinction of being the first congresswoman to be
granted a maternity leave while serving in the House. "I have
a stepdaughter who is nine and daughter of three. It's not
easy to be wife, mother, and politician. But I'm convinced,
first of all, that people do whatever is important to them. I'm
also of the opinion that you work it out. At this point in my
life, I recognize that it is a lot easier for me now than it may

be four years from now. I'm planning for that now. My baby will be of school age then. But I'm convinced that it can work, if you schedule and plan ahead. There's nothing wrong with individuals dealing with problems and developing suitable lifestyles. I'm fortunate in that during the period in which I married and became a mother, people were beginning to develop new lifestyles. There is more acceptance of multiple roles." The congresswoman pauses and continues with a serious expression on her face. "Also, I am fortunate to have a husband who is supportive and wanted me to run in the first place. Both of us are aware of potential difficulties and are planning for them now." Mr. William Burke, a businessman, lives in Los Angeles. He is politically astute and has a political background.

The Congresswoman returns to her district twice a month. Her three-year-old daughter, Autumn Roxanne, lives with her in Washington and attends a nursery school. Christine is nine and lives in Los Angeles. Every other weekend, the family is happily reunited in shared family activities.

Since assuming office, Mrs. Burke has personally introduced over 20 bills and major amendments. Enacted into law was a bill which provided funds for the initial planning of a comprehensive West Coast mass transit system and extended federal aid to autistic children. "I'm happy about the amendment that I introduced to the Alaskan pipeline. This was sort of a new area of law. Although this was not a government project, the Alaskan pipeline would be built on lands that are leased from the federal government to private enterprise. I felt that those private companies needed an affirmative action program for giving out contracts, as well as offering full employment to minorities and women. It was very late in getting started. There was no ready mechanism set up internally for carrying it out, but we were able to get about $250 million in contracts for minorities and women." She pauses to look at her watch and continues. "The essence of this amendment has since become an integral clause in various pieces of legislation, such as the Alaskan Natural Gas Transportation Act which covers the construction of a natural gas pipeline."

Another bill introduced by Congresswoman Burke has stirred national interest. "I'm spending a lot of time on my Equal Opportunity for the Displaced Homemakers Act. This bill, if passed, would provide federally subsidized training for women who have spent their lives as homemakers or housewives. Divorce, death, and abandonment by spouse have left this group without adequate economic support. A system of training and retraining would make them employable and self-supporting. The bill also calls for examining the feasibility of displaced homemakers receiving unemployment compensation."

Mrs. Burke finds that one of the unpleasant aspects of being a political figure is the public image most citizens have of them. "Right now there is so much criticism of people in public life. It's hard to accept the idea that one works so hard and people think you're dallying and loafing at the taxpayers' expense. 'You're being paid an outlandish salary and all you do is sit and enjoy life' seems to be the accusation. People should know of the way we have to run around and make great sacrifices to get the job done. At times, it's very depressing!"

One of the President Carter's expectations from the 95th Congress was a new ethics code to limit outside earnings of congressional members. The most intense debates in both the House and Senate on this issue centered on the provision that would limit a legislator's outside earnings to $8,625, or 15 percent of his official salary. The debates drew attention to the importance of outside income to members of Congress and pointed out some important differences in the ways that they earn it.

In the Senate, the central issue was honorariums for speaking engagements. Although Senators' six-year terms diminish their need to maintain outside business and professional ties, their prestigious titles afford them a built-in source of income. Since there are only 100 Senators, compared with 435 Representatives, each is in demand as a paid public speaker. Senator Edward Muskie, Democrat of Maine, for example, has earned almost $30,000 annually in previous years from the lecture circuit.

Most Senators maintain that honorariums from speaking engagements are an innocuous form of earnings. But there is a widely held belief that they amount to a disguised form of political gift. Critics of the honorarium system contend that while there are Senators such as Daniel P. Moynihan, Democrat of New York, and S. I. Hayakawa, Republican of California, whose performances on the podium might be worth $2,500, many others command similar fees without much evidence of oratorical skill. The Senate has placed a limitation on these fees to $25,000 annually for each Senator.

In the House, the ethics debate centered on business and professional connections maintained by members in their districts, reflecting the different position of Representatives. Serving relatively brief terms of two years, Representatives live in constant danger of being ousted from their seats and so tend, more than Senators, to retain their interests in businesses, farms, banks, and law firms back home.

Perhaps the outside activity most likely to lead to abuse is providing professional services. A survey taken in the last Congress disclosed that at least 53 members of the House earned more than $1,000 in the private practice of law. The Obey Commission, which drew up the new ethics rules for the House, estimated that between fifty and seventy-five members received more than $5,000 in 1975 for "personal services," and presumably most of those were lawyers. A member of Common Cause maintains that "selling personal services is an open avenue for abuse" because clients may think, perhaps justifiably, they are purchasing political influence when they go to a law firm whose letterhead bears the name of a member of Congress.

At the moment, whatever conflicts or abuses may exist remain hidden because there is no requirement that members of Congress disclose the exact amount or sources of their outside income. The new rule, which passed the House 344 to 79, requires the disclosure of sources as well as limiting the amount to 15 percent of salary. Even under the limits, Congressional members can earn either $66,000 or $72,000 annually.

Congresswoman Burke talks about her future. "I really don't know. . . . My own feeling is that I'm not temperamentally suited to stay here for a long period of time. I would really like to serve in the Senate, even for one term. I don't see that in my future in view of the present situation in California. I'm seriously considering running for a state-wide office— either lieutenant governor or attorney general of California. But I won't decide that for another year."

The conversation is interrupted by the ringing of the telephone. The caller reminds Mrs. Burke that she is expected on the floor of the House. She promises to meet the caller in the Rayburn Room.

In the course of her tenure on the Appropriations Committee, the congresswoman has been very active in fighting for increased funding for the Community Relations Service in the Department of Justice so that local jurisdictions might be more effectively aided in complying with court-ordered desegregation. She has been the leading advocate for the new Legal Services Corporation, which seeks to ensure the availability of resources for legal services and policy-level participation by women and minorities in its activities. Mrs. Burke has also been the leading proponent for the maintenance of funds for federal housing, the Small Business Administration, and other urban-oriented programs.

Congresswoman Burke serves on the board of directors of the United Negro College Fund, the American Civil Liberties Union Americans for Democratic Action, the National Athletic Health Institute, and numerous other organizations. She is also a member of the board of trustees of the University of Southern California, a trustee of the University of West Los Angeles, and a member of the UCLA Foundation. She is a life member of the National Council of Negro Women and a member of Alpha Kappa Alpha Sorority.

Before running off, she offers this advice to young women. "There are three things I would like them to consider seriously. The first one is—never allow a stereotype to measure your life. I think you just decide what your abilities are—what *you* would like to do. Even if you've never heard of anyone who looks like you or acts like you do who has done that, just do it! If you want to aspire to be governor, secretary of state or whatever, it's all right. It doesn't matter that you've never seen anyone that you can relate to in the job. Secondly —don't think you have limited alternatives . . . a choice between a career and motherhood. That's not true! Today you can do both things or you can say, 'at various times in my life, I'll do various things.' And don't think when you've made a decision it's forever. You may want to be an actress one year, a lawyer the next, a hair stylist, or a housewife. People change their professions at different times in their lives. They make choices when they're young, make different ones in the middle years, and may change again later on. And lastly, the most important thing is to get the kind of education which will permit flexibility and alternatives. And please don't forget basic skills of writing, speaking, and reading—they're vital!"

When Mrs. Burke has a little time away from the chores

of a congresswoman, she plays tennis and enjoys cooking. Time is so valued that just eating out becomes an occasion. "We have a boat, so we spend a lot of time on the ocean." She glances with eyes full of love at a picture of two adorable young girls. The picture rests on her desk. "These are my babies—even the little one enjoys boating." Congresswoman Burke shakes hands with a firm grip. It has been a long day for her. There was an early meeting with the Teacher of the Year who came by to see her representative. Her day is not over. When the meetings are finished, there's all that reading material to study for tomorrow's contests in the political arena.

Shirley Chisholm

The air was appropriately chilly for a November day. My appointment was for 10:30 A.M., but I arrived early. I wanted to see Restoration Plaza—one of the many projects sponsored by the late Senator Robert Kennedy in the Bedford Stuyvesant section of Brooklyn, New York. It seemed odd that the office of Congresswoman Chisholm—symbolic of the new—should be located in this reconstructed, historic site. But Mrs. Chisholm is a blend of the old and the new. Discipline, morality, dignity, and perseverance are characteristic of the old mores. Tenacity, outspokenness, purposefulness, and determination represented the new. The "Fighting Shirley Chisholm" label has been earned with pride.

Her physical measurements are surprising, for she is petite —a size five dress. Her vigorous handshake, spirited speech, and bright eyes project inner strength—the kind of strength that has sustained her since 1964. That was the year she made her debut into the political arena.

Shirley Anita St. Hill Chisholm, the oldest of four girls, was born in Bedford Stuyvesant on November 30, 1924. She attended Girls High School in Brooklyn where she excelled in French. Upon graduation, she enrolled in Brooklyn College to study early childhood education. Mrs. Chisholm earned her B.A. degree with cum laude honors. She continued her interest in education at Columbia University, and earned an M.A. degree and a professional diploma in the area of administration and supervision. To make her talents more relevant to the needs of the changing community, she studied Spanish and became fluent in speaking and writing it.

Mrs. Chisholm worked as a nursery school teacher for seven years, and later served as director of a private school for another five. Her interest in and concern for the health and social development of young children led to her position as educational consultant in the Division of Day Care, Bureau of Child Welfare. She was associated with that bureau for more than five years. In 1957, Mrs. Chisholm was the recipient of an award for outstanding work in the field of child welfare given by the Women's Council of Brooklyn. Her education and training have made her sensitive to the needs of all children and especially the needs of those who are poor and of minority origin. This concern increased her involvement in all aspects of day care and education of children. She voices this concern today with, "I don't believe that a woman with young children should work. Those first six to eight years of a child's life are so important! It is the time when values and personal characteristics are developed that influence the rest of one's life. Unless there is dire need, mothers should remain with their children."

In 1964, Mrs. Chisholm became Assemblywoman Chisholm with her election to the New York State Legislature. Membership on the Education, Health, and Social Welfare and Relief Committees permitted her to continue the fight for deprived children and their families. "Items in the state budget are listed according to priority—the most important first," she explained. "When the budget gets cut, the legislators start at the bottom—and year after year—child and social welfare bills are at the bottom of the list."

Assemblywoman Chisholm sought help for bills that would improve the state's child welfare system. She supported the idea of day care and extended use of day schools. "Many mothers of families on welfare want to work," she remarked, "but they have no one to care for their children which would free them to hold a job. We need to enable low-income families to help themselves." She joined others in the fight to liberalize adoption laws. Other states were moving ahead of New York in recognizing the minimal effect of differences in race and religion when all other aspects were positive. Many children spend their entire pre-adolescent years moving from one foster home to another. Good foster parents should be eligible to become adoptive parents.

Mrs. Chisholm's interest extended to other reform measures such as inspection of factories to ensure compliance with child labor laws. She demanded children twelve to fourteen years old be eliminated from organized migrant work forces. Her knowledge of the dreary, dull, home life which can retard learning motivated her to advocate mandatory kindergarten attendance for disadvantaged youngsters.

Although many people consider welfare families lazy and indifferent, Mrs. Chisholm has never taken this negative viewpoint. "Welfare families must be given the tools to earn their own way. Emphasis must be on training so that more of our citizens can feel pride in contributing to society," she contends.

Out of fifty bills introduced in the legislature by Mrs. Chisholm, eight passed. This is a significant score, considering the hundreds of bills introduced at each session and how few even reach the floor. She was especially pleased with one which created SEEK. This program made it possible for young men and women from poverty backgrounds to go to college. Supportive services of remedial, tutorial, and financial assistance helped them to remain and graduate. Another success was a bill to set up the state's first unemployment insurance coverage for personal and domestic employees. During her first year, one of her bills passed which pleased all female school-teachers. They would no longer lose their tenure rights if pregnancy interrupted their teaching careers.

Four years in Albany was excellent preparation for what was yet to come. She considered these years equivalent to a graduate course in politics. Much of what she learned made her sad. She saw that frequently one could not follow personal desires or convictions, but that one is forced to take another position because of the political dynamics. A person might be against a bill, but a telephone call in the middle of the night from a powerful figure delivering a veiled warning of the potential brevity of one's political future could cause a reversal in position. Mrs. Chisholm learned, too, that if a person follows his or her convictions which may provide the party with little political advantage, he or she must be ready to bear the consequences of this act and not complain. There is little consideration given to the independent thinker.

It was another redistricting that made it possible for Mrs. Chisholm to run for the United States Congress. Past practices of gerrymandering split the black vote into four districts so that the vote was ineffectual. The party leaders did not choose her, so she had to campaign the hard way . . . street by street among people desperately in need of change. Her slogan, "Fighting Shirley Chisholm—Unbought and Unbossed," gave them renewed hope and her the primary win. In the November 1968 election, she drew 34,885 votes to her chief rival, James Farmer's 13,777. The support of women's groups and Spanish-speaking residents had done it. Mrs. Chisholm's Spanish minor at Brooklyn College had been a good investment.

Her constituency is the 12th Congressional District whose center is Bedford Stuyvesant—an area of urban decay. This is New York's and perhaps the nation's largest ghetto. Her district also includes parts of Bushwick, East New York, and the Greenpoint communities. Blacks and Puerto Ricans compose more than 70 percent of the population. The rest are Jewish, Polish, Ukranian, and Italian. No other congressional district in Brooklyn is so diversified in its population.

Since she is such a well-organized and disciplined person, the freshman congresswoman was surprised at the informality of the opening of the 91st session of Congress. To begin with, Mrs. Chisholm broke an old House rule by arriving late. She had to return to the cloak room to deposit her hat and coat before taking the oath. Members walked around shaking hands, slapping each other on the back, and talking without paying any attention to the proceedings. Even the brief speeches were drowned out by the din. After each speech, a copy was handed to the clerk so it could be printed in full into the *Congressional Record*. Only those present would know how little had been said and how few even listened.

Every congressman is assigned to a committee. Some are more prestigious than others, but seniority determines one's chances. Democrats in the House delegate the assignment of members to committees to the Ways and Means Committee. The Republicans make use of a special Committee on Committees to perform the same task.

Because of Congresswoman Chisholm's twenty years of experience in education and work on educational legislation in the New York Assembly, she preferred the Education and Labor Committee. To her surprise and disappointment, she was assigned to the Agriculture Committee. Since this committee has jurisdiction over food stamp and surplus food programs and is concerned with migrant labor, she felt the assignment was still somewhat relevant to her constituents' needs and interests. But her subcommittee assignments were in the areas of rural development and forestry. She found this unacceptable.

"I really didn't know Speaker McCormack. But he had been gracious enough to repeat the swearing-in ceremony before a group of my friends and neighbors at the Capitol Hill Hotel. There were so many guests of freshman congressmen that this group couldn't be seated in the visitors' gallery and missed the official ceremony. I spoke to him about my committee and subcommittee assignments and asked for a change. He reminded me that this was traditional and one had to work and earn a reward of assignment of choice. I thought that I had always been a good soldier for all of my forty-three years. So I warned him that if there were no changes that I would have 'to do my own thing.' He didn't understand the expression, but he promised to consult with Wilbur Mills, chairman of the Ways and Means Committee."

The Congresswoman smiles slightly and clears her throat before beginning. "Mr. Mills didn't appreciate hearing about a complaining freshman member. And the fact that I had spoken directly to the speaker angered him further. But they did agree to look into the matter. In Congress, committee assignments are approved by the full Democratic or Republican majority at a caucus. As a novice, I sought advice from some of the more experienced members on how I could get the matter resolved satisfactorily. They warned me of the difficulties in even gaining recognition to make a motion. But I was not to be deterred."

Congresswoman Chisholm rises and moves quickly from behind her desk. "It was like a play," she begins. "You see— senior members are recognized first. So I was not to be recognized. Every time I tried to speak, a senior member would stand and be recognized. Some men were laughing and enjoying the farce, but I was not. So I walked toward the speaker's dais and stood there before Mr. Mills. He was startled but conferred with the majority leader, Carl Albert of Oklahoma. After a few moments, I was recognized by Mr. Mills. 'For what purpose is the gentlewoman from New York standing in the well?' "

The congresswoman looks grim. "I told him that he had failed to recognize me, although I had tried for more than one-half hour . . . perhaps he couldn't see me? I reminded the members of my experience as an educator and service on the Education Committee of the New York Assembly. I understood the role that seniority and geography played in assignments. But I asked the committee to think of the needs of the many blacks and Latins who elected me and the relevancy of my assignment. I reminded them of the percentages of the population that are black and Hispanic and how those percentages were under-represented in Congress. The House leadership had a moral commitment to attempt to correct that balance by putting the nine minority members in positions where they can work effectively. This kind of positive movement would go a long way toward helping this nation meet the critical problems of racism, deprivation, and urban decay. They listened politely. And then I suggested a reconsideration of my assignments through an amendment. This procedure was not in accord with parliamentary procedure, and Mr. Mills asked me to withdraw it. He assured me that recognition on the floor would be possible at another time. He kept his word and the amendment passed. Afterwards several male members of Congress expressed sympathy for me and my future. They felt that I had committed political suicide." But Mrs. Chisholm learned later that her courage had been admired by almost everyone including the old-time politicians.

As a freshman congresswoman, Mrs. Chisholm saw her role extending into two directions. The primary one would be any activity which could help her constituents. This kind of practical help is called a "case load" in Capitol Hill terminology. This means all the problems for which citizens seek help from their representatives. These include, among other things, problems in housing, discrimination in employment, unjust imprisonment, citizenship, and education. Her second role would be to use her office to apply pressure at the federal level to get grants and programs for her district. In this way, she would also combat much of the discrimination involved in federal contracts which help to build schools, highways, housing complexes, and hospitals.

Congresswoman Chisholm's files reveal how well she has carried out that role:

CASE A: An elderly woman, ailing and under hospital treatment, faced cutoff of her social security and Medicare benefits, her role source of income, through a technicality. Her problem was brought to the attention of Representative Chisholm whose office got in touch with appropriate officials in the Social Security Administration and other federal agencies. After considerable consultation, an arrangement was worked out to overcome the technicality and the old woman's benefit payments were restored.

CASE B: A young serviceman, on orders to report to a base abroad for duty, was concerned about his wife in Brooklyn. She had lost one child, was expecting again, and it was feared the strain of separation from her husband at such a time might have ill results. A letter from the congresswoman's office urging, if possible, a "compassionate reassignment," won favorable consideration, and the young serviceman was given a one-year reassignment to Fort Dix, New Jersey, where he could be reasonably near his wife for at least the twelve-month period.

CASE C: A naturalized citizen, concerned about the long delay in processing his wife's application in Haiti for an immigrant visa, enlisted Representative Chisholm's help. Through direct contact with the United States Embassy in Haiti, issuance of the visa was expedited.

CASE D: A retired USAF member sought help to find out why he was not receiving his retirement checks. Upon inquiry from the congresswoman's office, the Department of the Air Force investigated, located the checks, and forwarded them to the retiree, who finally was able to report that he was receiving all of his checks regularly.

CASE E: A native Czechoslovakian woman with relatives in Brooklyn was having great difficulty overcoming government opposition to her request for an exit visa to emigrate to this country. Her plight was brought to Mrs. Chisholm's attention. Her office, working through the U.S. State Department, was able, after considerable effort, to help influence the Czechoslovakian government to grant the visa.

CASE F. Disturbed about the poor quality of postal service in his area, a local citizen reported that on several occasions mail dropped in the mailbox was still in the box two or three days later. Attempts to correct the situation on his own had proven futile, he said. In his behalf, a request was made of the U.S. Postal Service National Office, Washington, D.C., for a full investigation of the man's complaint. The Postal Service verified the charges, promised immediate steps to rectify the situation, and advised that there would be official reprimands to those individuals responsible for the poor quality of service.

Congresswoman Chisholm's success in bringing federal aid to community residents is confirmed by this excerpt from a letter from CABS (the Consumer Action Program of Bedford Stuyvesant):

> We would like to express our appreciation for all your efforts on our behalf during the last several years. Your assistance has been instrumental in bringing hundreds of thousands of contract dollars into our agency. These monies have helped to:
>
> Develop $8 million in physical developmental projects such as nursing homes and housing developments which provided essential services and employment opportunities to area residents.
>
> Develop a CABS Credit Union which has provided over $3 million in low cost loans to residents.
>
> Develop and operate housekeeper services which earn needed community investment capital and provide employment for 400 residents.
>
> Attract more than $555,000 in private, outside capital into the Bedford Stuyvesant community.

The agency expressed much gratitude for the congresswoman's constant encouragement and inspiration which motivated the group to strive and expand its efforts to promote neighborhood revitalization and growth.

Congresswoman Chisholm respects and urges upward mobility for others as well as herself. When she announced her candidacy for president of the United States in 1972, most people thought she was crazy. Her colleagues knew her as a maverick but couldn't believe that she would go so far. It was obvious that she couldn't get the nomination and didn't need the humiliation of trying and losing. Yet, despite the tremendous expenditure of time and energy, she found the venture worthwhile. She reasoned that there was a pressing need for change in politics, particularly in presidential elections. The disenfranchised people of this country, heretofore, never had a voice in the political decision-making process. They needed to be heard; they needed a voice. After much soul-searching, the congresswoman chose to be that voice. "I have blazed a trail, and that was my intention. I was, am, and always will be, a catalyst for change. And as more and more women begin to participate in the political process, we will see the visible effect of that change," she says with feeling. She wrote a book recounting her experiences as a presidential candidate called *The Good Fight.*

This congresswoman has served on the important House Subcommittee on Equal Opportunities, sponsored a bill designed to save O.E.O. (Office of Educational Opportunity), and fought to keep New York City from losing $50 million under Title I of the Elementary and Secondary Educational Act. These are just a few of her many accomplishments over the past eight years.

Women enter the career of politics by various routes. The congresswoman traces her initial interest in politics to a course completed as a sophomore at Brooklyn College. The course included volunteer work in the community—specifically in the areas of English and Spanish remedial and tutorial assistance. For the first time, she understood the wonderful satisfaction to be gained by working directly with people. Just the contact with another person helped to lift some of the residents out of despair and desolation, even though it may have been momentary. "For young people seeking careers in politics, volunteer work in their local neighborhoods or communities will give them a sense of involvement in various lifestyles," Mrs. Chisholm advises. "They get to understand the needs of the people firsthand also."

When she made the decision to associate herself totally with local politics, her friends were dismayed and confused.

She was a successful educator and respected in the community—why leave all of that for a career in a field in which she would only find rejection. Even then, in that pre-women's liberation era of eighteen or nineteen years ago, the congresswoman felt the need for women to move away from their traditional roles. She has always advocated that any person with certain attributes that can be utilized to ameliorate the misery of humanity should use them. Why not try? "I've always been game. So I accepted the challenge."

Looking back over the years as assemblywoman and congresswoman, Mrs. Chisholm ascribes her effectiveness to several talents. "First, one must be able to express oneself —skillful articulation is vital for anyone aspiring to public life. The next factor in importance is the art of liking people. Often this is quite difficult, because people have unpleasant lives, particularly those in need. People with whom you must work are often motivated by selfish reasons, but you have to deal with that too. But if you hope to represent them, you must expect and accept the good with the bad. A prospective politician needs extraordinary strength. Frustration and turbulence can cause one's energy to be at a very low ebb. But the light that shines from a child's or older person's eyes whom you've helped gives one renewed strength and the vitality to go on. This is very true for me," she says softly. Finally, Congresswoman Chisholm recommends tremendous self-confidence. "This is particularly needed for women. People are waiting to take pot shots at you, but if you feel that you have something to give and like the art—this profession permits one to make a unique contribution."

Today women have much to offer their communities and it behooves them to utilize these assets with the courage of their convictions and render vital services. The congresswoman continues. "Contrary to accepted legend, few women are in community or political service for monetary rewards. Their participation hinges on a sincere desire to be of service to people on every level. Women want and need intellectual stimuli beyond their own four walls: to be challenged by a job; to develop their talents; and to gain satisfaction in learning, earning, and doing something more. Women do not desire to be aggressive, that is, to be like men. They want to be themselves and political activists by gentle persuasion."

As to the special contribution women can make, Mrs. Chisholm provides these comments. "Women seem to possess specific talents to a greater degree than men. For example, women historically have developed a reservoir of inner strengths, perseverence, tolerance, and patience just through the lives they've led." Women have innate and unique qualities that men don't possess. "Specifically in the area of principles and morality," she explains. "There is a tendency for women to be more concerned and aware of 'what is right' and 'what is wrong.' This may be due to the scarcity of women in politics. Women have had neither the opportunity nor the temptations in the decision-making process. Perhaps in years to come, women will behave more like men, particularly as more women go into politics. I hope this doesn't happen. But the field needs more 'positive images.' Young people are turned off by the unethical and blatant sinful practices of politicians in recent years."

Although women work at responsible jobs, head households, and can be seen almost everywhere, many people still feel that woman's place is in the home. The congresswoman feels that, in Washington at least, attitudes are changing. "After eight years in Congress, I've seen many changes. Once you've proved yourself, the men respect you. As a matter of fact, they seek you out for help with their legislation . . . not publicly, of course." Mrs. Chisholm says with a sly grin. "But men appreciate and respect a woman's ability to deal with the issues."

Congresswoman Chisholm believes her greatest political achievement was the battle to get domestics under the National Labor Relation Act so that they could receive the federal minimum wage. Approximately 85 percent of domestics are minority women. If they had not been covered, they would continue to be exploited in several sections of the country. She feels very proud of this accomplishment.

Many women are wives, mothers, and full-time career persons. "This is a very difficult role. I often wonder how women with young children can be full-time politicians, wives, and mothers—you have to be all three—and there are so many demands! You have to go to lunches, dinners, make speeches, run to work, and serve your constituents. As much as I enjoy my career, I don't believe that I would have become a political person if I had young children. One reason is that I love young children too much. I truly believe the first eight years of a child's life should be with the parent or mother. Unless, of course, financial necessity demands that the parent be out of the home. Having said that, there are young women in Congress who do manage. They are fortunate enough to be married to understanding husbands—liberated men. There are no 'male tasks' or 'female tasks' in their homes. Each washes dishes, cooks, or changes diapers. Others are fortunate enough to have full-time household help or governesses. But there are some who have difficult strains and stresses in their marriages. This is understandable, because a politician's life is a very demanding kind of life." Mrs. Chisholm pauses for a moment. "I guess all of us try to find various ways of working it out. Some of us are successful and some are not. You realize that it is quite different from being a lawyer, banker, or stockbroker. These careers permit a woman to work regular hours and spend evenings with her family. But a politician's day never ends. It is possible to speak at two lunches, see constituents, attend three meetings, receive an award at a dinner, and chair several committees, all within eighteen hours, and in more than one state."

The congresswoman has this advice for young people

seeking careers in politics. "If she is a girl who is rather shy and sensitive, then she should seek out a different kind of career. A girl must have a well developed sense of self-confidence. She must be able to take it! It might sound strange, but since I am a religious person, you must have a tremendous faith in God. And I do! I'm a very religious woman and not ashamed to say so. After some of the hardships that I've conquered, I must believe that God charted this life for me. Without that faith, I would have become totally destroyed—really stark, raving mad."

Mrs. Chisholm's final words were these. "I am certain that more and more American women want to become more involved in politics. It could be the salvation of our nation. If there were more women in politics, it would be possible to start cleaning it up! Women I have known in government have seemed to me to be much more apt to act for the sake of a principle or moral purpose. They are not as likely as men to engage in deals, manipulations, and sharp tactics. A large proportion of women in Congress and every other legislative body would serve as a reminder that the real purpose of politicians is to work for the people."

On January 19, 1977, Congresswoman Chisholm was given a seat on the influential House Rules Committee by the Democratic caucus. She became the second woman in history to be so honored. To the press she commented, "I think it was because of my ability to work with different groups and because I'm articulate and rather persuasive. So somebody said, 'Let's put the gal on.' "

In joining the Rules Committee, which decides when bills move to the floor, Mrs. Chisholm said that being a moderate progressive means she'll bring another added dimension to the committee. She'll also be in a position to push for early action on social, education, and antipoverty legislation dealing with people who have been voiceless and powerless. "I can have much more clout," she concluded.

Cardiss Collins

Pictures of her that hang in the outer office do not capture the natural beauty of this lively congresswoman. Today someone has distributed bubble gum to all of the offices and everyone is chewing away. "I'm trying to get rid of this sweet taste in my mouth. I've been sampling the bubble gum, too!" She laughs good naturedly. Her handshake is firm and extended, as she welcomes the intrusion into her busy day.

Mrs. Collins is among those congresswomen who filled a seat left vacant upon the death of a husband. Campaigning for a House seat was a natural sequence of events in her life, however, because she had been deeply involved in her husband's commitments. "I always tell young people in Chicago that they must prepare themselves for more than one career in life. Today a person can look forward to several careers, as interests grow and change and one matures. Several careers might offer challenge from different aspects at different times in one's life."

She settles herself comfortably behind the large desk and continues. "I was not educated to be a congresswoman, but then no one goes to school to become a member of Congress. As for my preparation, I was interested in accounting, but began as a stenographer with the Illinois Department of Labor. I progressed through the ranks to become an accountant in the Illinois Department of Revenue, Eventually I moved into the position of revenue auditor. My government service at the state level amounted to twenty-two years."

Mrs. Collins was not political at all. Her husband, George, was considered to be the family politician. "He was alderman and ward committeeman before gaining a seat in Congress. But, as his wife, I was exposed to the political climate and those people who were very influential in Chicago's political arena. I accompanied him to various dinners and receptions where I met important people. When he decided to run, we held strategy sessions on how to get him press coverage and make him known. We planned and composed letters, leaflets and other publicity materials for his campaign. So by the time he announced his candidacy for Congress, we were seasoned. The only difference was his constituency. The 6th Congressional District in which he first ran was composed of less than 50 percent black people—Berwyn and Cicero. This added a new dimension, because the local politics are quite different from those of an entire congressional district. It took a great deal of ingenuity, good solid politics, and the strength of the Democratic Party to win support. So I was a vital part of all of his struggles and victories over a ten-year period. It took him that long to rise from city council to the House of Representatives." Congresswoman Collins stops to clear her throat. She has been speaking in her usual brisk, concise manner.

George Collins was successful in his campaign for United

States Representative of the 6th and, finally, of the 7th Districts of Illinois. Mrs. Collins was his most trusted confidant and chief ally. While he served his constituency in Congress, she was the behind-the-scene strategist. One would think that upon his sudden and tragic death, she would want his seat as a continuation of the life they shared. But this was not the case. "I really intended to stay home and continue my career as revenue auditor. This was my choice. But George's friends and mine, along with the Democratic Party organization, asked me to run to fill his unexpired term. But after I was elected, on June 5, 1973, something happened. I discovered that I liked it!" Her hearty laughter fills the quiet room.

In her first election, Congresswoman Collins won 87 percent of the vote and in the next election—85 percent. "It is my hope to do as well the next time around." She smiles. "But I'm really running on my own record—not just following in my husband's footsteps." Her own record is praiseworthy. She is the first woman and first black to chair the House Government Operations Subcommittee on Manpower and Housing. She also serves on that committee's Subcommittee on Commerce, Consumer, and Monetary Affairs. The congresswoman is a member of the International Relations Committee's Subcommittee on Africa as well as its Subcommittee on Inter-American Affairs. Although she became a member of the latter (formerly known as the House Committee on Foreign Affairs) during the last session of Congress, she has already earned the reputation of being a member who "does her homework." The House Democratic caucus recently assigned her to the District of Columbia Committee where she sits on the Judiciary Subcommittee.

Her ability to "get the job done" was recognized by the then House majority leader, Thomas P. "Tip" O'Neill, who on January 23, 1975, appointed her to become a whip-at-large—

the first black to ever hold that office within the leadership structure of the United States House of Representatives.

In August 1976, she was appointed an ex-officio member of the newly formed House Select Committee on Drug Abuse and Control and is the only woman to be named to serve thereon. During the 94th Congress, Congresswoman Collins was elected secretary of the Congressional Black Caucus; currently, she is treasurer of that body.

This congresswoman has sponsored more than twenty-five bills. Those highest on her priority list include the National Condominium Act, the Economic Disaster Community Assistance Act, and the Elementary and Secondary Education Act. Other areas of legislative interest involve bills to help the aged, consumer credit, Medicare, and water pollution.

One bill that evokes pleasant thoughts deals with the subject of breast prosthesis. This bill would permit prostheses to be a payable item under Medicare. Although the bill wasn't passed, the legislation drew enough attention so that the guideline was written to cover it within the Social Security Administration. Another bill concerned the problems we face in the inner-city. It is Bill H.R. 250 which says a child, aged three to five, can go to an educational center. In Chicago, these are called Child-Parent Centers. They have different names for them in other states. In Chicago, an unusual thing happened—many children at age five had reached reading readiness level or beyond. The result was a threat to abolish the program under Title I of the Education Act. I'm fighting now to keep that provision intact."

If one had to name the greatest handicap in the life of a member of Congress, it would be time. "You don't have the time to be with your family. Even if they're here in Washington, our hours are very long. For example, on any given morning, I have an 8:00 A.M. breakfast. From that breakfast,

I'll go into a meeting—perhaps a whip's meeting at 9:15 A.M. From that meeting, at 10:00 A.M. I'll go on to a sub-committee meeting which I chair. That's the manpower and housing meeting which would convene until noon. If the House goes into session at 11:00 A.M., then I'll be racing back and forth between meetings and the Capitol. It's important for me to know the issues as they are discussed on the floor and to have my opinions recorded. In the afternoon, there are series of appointments to be kept. In the evenings, there's usually a reception or dinner which lasts several hours. By the time you get home, it's 10:00 P.M. Of course, there are still letters to be signed, meetings with office staff, constituents, and visitors, and finally the reading and studying for tomorrow."

Congresswoman Collins feels that the greatest obstacle to progress, for men as well as women, is apathy. "I suppose Chicago only reflects what's happening all over the country. But young people don't vote! And that's the one thing anyone can do. There's no better way to participate in the system!"

Mrs. Collins has one son of seventeen years. "We have an extended family relationship. My mother supervises his care while I'm in Washington. When I arrive home, we take my mother to her own house. I then become a mother for the weekend!" Her face is radiant. She thinks for a moment and then continues in her rapid-fire pace. "You see . . . my mother had retired. Although she knew we all loved her, she had little to do. So this arrangement had several advantages. It gave her the opportunity to know that she is loved. I have always been a working mother. But now there's someone at home all the time. And my son enjoys being spoiled by a doting grandmother. I don't have to worry either, because I know he's getting the best of care." There is a picture of this good looking youngster near her desk.

Mrs. Collins has discussed a possible career in politics with Kevin. "But he doesn't show any inclination for this kind of life. In fact, for the last few years . . . he avoids any mention of it." She laughs at the thought. "My husband and I were the first black husband and wife team to come to Congress. But then—Kevin's only seventeen, so who can say?"

Congresswoman Collins serves her constituency in many ways. Through a postal patron service, she invites homemakers and residents of the 7th Congressional District of Illinois to send for free literature published by the United States Department of Agriculture. These pamphlets cover a wide variety of subjects like gardening, home freezing, meat and poultry, and home safety. Each request is answered and one may receive up to five bulletins by writing to her office.

There are also newsletters and reports from the congresswoman to her district. One report told of her impressions of life in China. She wrote—

At the end of our two-day mission in Ch'eng-tu, we went to Kweilin where we saw some of the world's most beautiful caves. On the first day, we visited a silk factory. Sixty-five percent of the 2400 workers who produce pongee silk, cotton silk, chemical fiber, and pure silk are women. Of these, 60 percent are cadres (in officer training).

After learning that the factory was unionized, I was interested in knowing the kinds of employee benefits or work-condition improvements it had been instrumental in obtaining. We found that many technical innovations had been implemented in the factory where the average pay for an eight-hour-day, six-day-week is roughly fifty yuan ($25) per month. Since the cost of living in the PRC (People's Republic of China) has remained stable while production has rapidly increased, wages, we were told, have risen more in purchasing power than in cash. When one considers that housing for a married couple who live in Kweilin in one room with kitchen privileges costs about $1 monthly, as does child care services, the average wage seems to be adequate.

A mother-to-be is allowed to work until her seventh month of pregnancy. During that time she is given one hour of rest during the work day. After childbirth, she is granted fifty-six days of maternity leave before returning to the factory where she is allowed one hour per day in which to feed the baby who has been placed in the factory nursery. It was interesting to note that while our babies are usually wrapped in blankets of white, pale blue, pink or yellow, the Chinese infant is wrapped in bright red clothes which is a gift of the state.

On March 22, 1977, the congresswoman's office issued a news release regarding improper United States arms transfer shipments to South Africa. She reported—"In 1976, the United States licensed nearly $300,000 worth of dangerous arms for export to the Republic of South Africa." These licensed arms shipments, including shotguns and rifles, are classified as "non-military" by the United States Department of Commerce. According to Mrs. Collins' research, this is in direct conflict with America's support of the 1963 United Nations resolution "to cease forthwith the sale and shipment of arms, ammunition of all types, and military vehicles to South Africa."

The congresswoman is today introducing a resolution calling for executive review of United States policies and practices on arms shipments to South Africa. White citizens are arming themselves to the teeth. One out of every four whites owns a gun in South Africa. Such a statistic is not surprising in a country where every white male high school student is required to study target shooting in preparation for what one can only surmise would be possible uprisings by the black majority. The congresswoman is a member of the House International Relations Subcommittee on Africa and has toured many sections of Africa, including her most recent trip to South Africa in November 1976. Mrs. Collins intends to hold subcommittee hearings on the subject of South Africa arms transfers and on her resolution in the near future.

Despite her congressional duties, Mrs. Collins manages to give service to professional, social, and community associations like her colleagues. She is vice–president of the Lawndale Youth Commission; a member of the First Baptist Church of Chicago, NAACP, the Chicago Urban League, National Council of Negro Women, and the National Women's Political Caucus; and an honorary member of Alpha Kappa Alpha Sorority and several other organizations.

She is listed in "Who's Who," "Who's Who Among Black Americans," "Who's Who in America," "Who's Who in Black America," and "Who's Who in Government" and is the recipient of numerous awards for her many outstanding accomplishments.

The future for women politicians holds many opportunities. It is wide open for those who want to take advantage of changing attitudes, according to Congresswoman Collins. She feels that there is a great amount of respect for each other among members of Congress. "Everyone stands on his or her merits. The male-female syndrome really doesn't exist here. You rarely hear, 'Oh she's thinking like a woman rather than a congresswoman.' As members of Congress, we represent everyone who lives in our districts. So we represent men and women, and must concentrate on issues and problems that concern all the people. When we vote on and pass legislation, it affects everyone in the nation. And that's a great responsibility."

Millicent Fenwick

She's tall with regal bearing. For a moment, you have a feeling that you've seen her picture on the society pages of *The New York Times*. Her stride is sure and confident. Well-groomed and elegantly attired, Millicent Fenwick still looks very much like an associate editor, her former vocation. But the moment she welcomes you into her private office, the congresswoman's cordial and relaxed attitude removes any fears you may have entertained about her aloofness. She is anything but stuffy. Congresswoman Fenwick is going to have a quick lunch at her desk and graciously asks me to join her. "Just milk and a sandwich," she says simply. "I'm not much of a lunch eater and there's always so little time anyway."

Congresswoman Fenwick represents the 5th District of New Jersey. Her career as a member of Congress began much later than the average member's. For years, she worked as an editor for the Conde Nast Publications chain. Yet she always maintained an interest in community and local politics. Her extensive background in elective office ranges from school board, to borough council, to state assembly. Service at each level afforded her a better view of the vast, complicated network which governs citizens' lives. In recognition of her work in consumer affairs, the governor of New Jersey appointed her director of New Jersey's Division of Consumer Affairs. In the spring of 1974, she resigned from this post to make a bid for the Republican nomination for Congress.

"It really happened in a most unorthodox way," she begins. "In my congressional district, we had had a very fine, honorable man for twenty-two years. He was young, with a long period of service, and there was no indication that he was not going to continue. But one day, one of the reporters who knew me when I served in the State Assembly came up to me and said, 'You'd better watch my column tomorrow.' And so I did. The next day, the column reported that this able congressman was considering not running, and the 'people' were talking about my running. Of course, nobody was talking about it!" She laughs at the memory. "And certainly I hadn't thought of it at all, because I didn't know he wasn't running. But that started the ball rolling. And soon other people throughout the state were talking about it. The more I thought about it, the more interesting it seemed. I had noticed many areas in my consumer's position which involved federal legislation, such as bankruptcy. And I thought perhaps I can be useful in consumer affairs.

"So I ran in a very hotly contested primary against two male opponents. And I won in a tremendous landslide by eighty-four votes," the Congresswoman tosses her head backward and enjoys a hearty laugh. "Of course, there was a recount, and it turned out the same way . . . exactly a margin of eighty-four votes." Her eyes light up and she grins impishly, before taking another bite of her sandwich. "And then I ran in the general election, where I had three masculine opponents. But it was worth it and most stimulating! And frankly, I prefer elective to appointed jobs. Because nobody has favored you. You stand with your people and are judged by your relationship with them. It's a wonderful feeling and makes you feel part of the whole system. And we are brothers and sisters—there's nothing like elective office that makes it more clear. And I find that enormously comforting."

You almost stare at her in admiration. What does it take to make a person assume such a horrendous yet rewarding career at the age of sixty-four? "There's no question about it. This is the best job I've ever had in my life," Congress-woman Fenwick says in her husky voice. In her freshman year, 1975, she was appointed to the Committees on Bank-ing, Currency and Housing and the Small Business Commit-tee. On the Banking Committee, she has made the following legislative contributions: an amendment requiring banks to pay the consumer's legal fees if the bank does not correctly estimate the final cost of a lease and must go to court to re-solve the matter; and an amendment under the Fair Credit Billing Act rendering the advisory opinions of federal agen-cies legally binding, thereby protecting small businessmen who must rely on these interpretations of the law. Congresswoman Fenwick also proposed the amendment permitting creditors to give preference to older Americans under the Equal Credit Opportunity Act; and an amendment exempting small banks from certain costly, record-keeping procedures. She con-sistently fights for good, clean government. This articulate member of Congress says, "Life isn't fair, and we may have to accept that in some ways, but wherever possible, govern-ment must be our collective approach to correcting inequi-ties. We must concern ourselves with justice at all levels."

As a congresswoman, Millicent Fenwick is well-known for her courage and fearlessness in challenging senior members on issues that conflict with her belief in integrity and common sense in government. She has openly and eloquently battled with them on matters of reform in elections and personal lulus (financial plums) for House members.

"I've been divorced for about thirty years now," Congress-woman Fenwick confides when talking about her family. "I have two children and eight grandchildren," she says like any proud grandmother. "You see—I worked for a while after the divorce. I became a Vogue model." Her figure hasn't changed much in all of those years either, and her carriage would make any fledgling model give up food for a year. "Later I wrote features for the magazine and even the *Vogue Book of Etiquette*." Working and mothering have always been blended comfortably into her lifestyle. "My daughter lives in North Carolina with her five children. So I really never saw a great deal of them anyway, even when I was consumer director in New Jersey. My son has been living abroad, but he's back now and recently re-married. So he's happy to have me out of his hair," she laughs in jest.

Although Congresswoman Fenwick favors ERA, she has some reservations. "There's one question I have about this women's liberation movement. I'm so afraid that it's not going to turn out to be liberation. I fear that everybody who wants to stay home and take care of a husband and children will feel guilty and diminished as a person." She folds her hands and leans back in the chair. She appears lost in thought, and then she says. "And really if you're going to judge things in the degree of difficulty . . . I have a friend, Bella Abzug, former congresswoman from New York. I used to say—'you have to look at her accomplishments. She's got two fine children. She is a lawyer and a member of Congress.' And I put them in the order of descending difficulty and achievement. Because it is really a grind getting a law degree. The responsibility of care and bringing up children plus a good marriage which means discipline, self-discipline and sacrifice every step of the way, are not easy feats," Congresswoman Fenwick declares sharply.

"I hope we're not going to get too locked into categories. Those who like to work outside of the family structure must be able to do so. It's absolutely outrageous to cripple those people. There's an advertisement that used to be around that read—'The Tragedy of a Wasted Mind.' It pictured this boy looking into your eyes and into the future and thinking of a wasted mind. It's a terrible thing . . . male or female. Each person has to make that decision which is best for her and her family—according to her personal nature. Many women have children and hold jobs and are successful at both." Millicent Fenwick's voice rises with passion.

Congresswoman Fenwick, like her colleagues, works long hours. On weekends and during congressional recesses, she returns to the 5th District to serve her supporters. This is one of the satisfactions of the job. Another plus is the opportunity to travel and broaden her understanding of international problems. In 1975, thirty-five nations, including the United States, signed the Final Act of the European Conference on Security and Cooperation, usually known as the Helsinki Accord. That summer Congresswoman Fenwick was part of a delegation from the House which went to Russia. She says, "The trip for me—a somewhat distant and theoretical exercise in international diplomacy—became a dramatically present and personal issue. I saw people in Russia and in Romania—the dissidents, the 'refuseniks,' the Jews, Baptists, Catholics, and Lutherans—the lost, helpless people, anxiously waiting for exit visas, for news of imprisoned husbands, for the next visit of the dreaded secret police. . . . Their faces are unforgettable." In her *Millicent Fenwick Reports,* she asked her constituents to support legislation, introduced by her, to protect and provide human rights leading to the reunification of families, freedom of movement, and freedom for journalists.

There are dissatisfactions, too, in being a member of Congress. Congresswoman Fenwick put it this way. "Oh well—there are terrible frustrations! You have a good idea, and somehow you can't get anybody to take it up. For instance, I've had an idea for years. I think it's a terrific idea! I have two, as a matter of fact." Her eyes twinkle. "One is for people who rent homes who ought to be able to get their rent deposit when the small claims court says they should have it. In New Jersey, we have a law that says the landlords have to tell you where your rent deposit is and what interest it's accumulating. Now I think that if you get a judgment from the small claims court remanding your deposit, as a tenant you ought to be able to go down with your piece of paper and retrieve it. You ought not to have to pay a constable or a lawyer to get back what is yours." She rests for a moment. "What got me started on this was a case where a woman spent days trying to get back $60.00. That money meant a lot to her," she explains.

"Now my other idea falls on deaf ears, too. When a criminal court has convicted a man of criminal fraud, at the state level, I see no reason why that same judge, court, and jury shouldn't go on to civil restitution. Now the usual procedure is the judge says—'you're guilty—sentence suspended'—and off he goes. But what about the victims? They must now, at their own expense, go to civil court for any restitution. The courts are jammed, the waiting time is long, and the expense is great. Why shouldn't the state undertake something for the individual? Why should victims have to retain a lawyer to regain their own property? The state ought to be on their side. This adversary position that the state has gotten itself into with its citizens is a bitter thing." She adds with deliberateness. "The search for justice dignifies man, and this must also be the dignity of our government." These are two of Congresswoman Fenwick's ideas, and, hopefully, someday soon other members of Congress will give them serious consideration.

When the long day is over, Mrs. Fenwick returns to her small house very near Capitol Hill. "I used to have hobbies like gardening and needlework, and they were my great resources. When my sister was alive, I went abroad to visit her for three to six weeks every winter. But I have no hobbies now." She adds, "I've been in a lot of jobs. But this is the most complete, because of the variety of subject areas—whether it's foreign affairs or forestry, taxes, energy, or whatever. It's fascinating! You sit there and really try. You listen to every debate. You follow every argument. You've read every report. And still you say where is the public good?"

When asked about the special talents women may have that government needs, the congresswoman responds with, "Although I don't really believe in group characteristics, I have noticed a few things. When I was in the state legislature, there were two bills. One was to cover the wetlands and the protection of the wetlands. It was proposed by a female legislator, Josephine Margetts. The other covered flood plains and the protection of the flood plains. This bill was mine. Now a lot of people had been in the legislature before we arrived, but when I came to the legislature she was the only female in the assembly. I was only there three years, but these bills which related to the needs of the land were proposed by women." She is reflective for several seconds.

"I've often said that if we'd had a woman president and a lot of female physicists, we probably wouldn't be on the moon. But I think we'd have really marvelous garbage recycling in every county all over the country—in all 3,000 of them. They'd be practical and highly technical, too. Our energies would just have taken another direction, you see. Men, when thinking of themselves, tend to borrow from A. W. E. O'Shaughnessy. Men always say that they are 'the music makers, the dreamers of dreams . . . the movers and shakers of the world forever it seems.' To some extent, this may be true. Well—movers and shakers we do need, but we also need some people who will question the practical and humane aspects of some of the sweeping legislation that is proposed. An example is the regulation which forbids children in senior citizen housing. How are grandparents ever going to see and play with their children? Women have more practical thoughts. Usually a masculine bill is quite complicated and involved with lawyers and process servers. The bill I mentioned earlier—involving landlord and tenant— is a typical female bill. Another example is the Food Stamp Program. It took Leonor Sullivan four years to get it through the committee. It was a realistic way of using up surplus food products and getting them to the people who needed them."

Congresswoman Fenwick has introduced other legislation that's significant. One was the bill to amend the bankruptcy laws to protect consumer creditors. Under the present law, consumer creditors are listed last in the order of priority and stand very little chance of recovering the goods or services for which they have paid when a business goes bankrupt. Low income consumers are especially vulnerable because they are more apt to shop on credit in financially marginal neighborhood stores. For them, the loss of a $500 deposit can be tragic. This bill would give consumer creditors standing in the bankruptcy proceedings. The bill was first introduced in June 1975, and has been reintroduced in the 95th Congress with fifty-eight co-sponsors.

She mentions her other interests. "Through hearings and investigations in my small business committee work, I became aware of the need to modify excessive and outdated ICC regulations affecting the trucking industry. Reform in this area is critical to promote competition within the industry and benefit the consumer who is presently paying the cost of this regulation.

"Legislation I am preparing would: (1) ease entry requirements to stimulate competition and promote increased pricing flexibility, and (2) create federal standards in those areas where conflicting state regulations place unnecessary and costly burdens on the interstate carriers.

"I have had extensive correspondence with the chairman of the ICC in which many of these questions and problems were raised. The material and information which accumulated has been turned over to the Council on Wage and Price Stability for an economic analysis of the inflationary effects of this regulation and the ultimate cost this imposes on the consumers. The material has also been turned over to the Justice Department for their investigation."

The congresswoman reaches for reports on her desk. "I am preparing a bill to compensate those who have contracted 'asbestos-related' diseases as a result of occupational exposure to asbestos. The preliminary work has been very encouraging as I have been working closely with both the union and the management of a major United States asbestos manufacturer, as well as consulting with the leading medical expert in this area."

This charming sixty-seven-year-old woman is as profound as an ancient sage and as young in spirit as a teenager. Witty, honest, and direct, she wears her pacemaker as easily as one wears a ring. Her stamina seems endless. The congresswoman's pipe smoking does not appear to be a contradiction of her urbane, sophisticated femininity. It just adds to her uniqueness.

"I think young people shouldn't spend so much time trying to find themselves. They complain of not knowing themselves, who they are, or are undergoing identity crises. What I've discovered about life is that you really ought not to think too much about yourself. Somewhere in the Bible it says, 'He who loses himself finds himself' or words to that effect. And that's true! Whether you're interested in photography, marine biology, basketball, human rights, music, or whatever . . . just go out and do it. Get involved and you don't have to worry about who you are. Everything falls into place. It's like aerodynamics. The moment you have a direction, you get shape."

Congresswoman Fenwick has found herself and is a real inspiration to whomever is lucky enough to know her.

Marjorie Holt

It happens frequently—a teacher will influence the entire life of a student. It happened to Marjorie Sewell Holt in the seventh grade. "I had a very fine civics teacher who discussed careers and vocations with the class. She advised me about the possibilities of a law career as a way to express my interests and talents. Even at that tender age, I knew that I wanted to be a member of the House of Representatives." Mrs. Holt laughs softly, as she remembers. "Of course, I had to set aside my ambition many, many times during my life, but the desire was always there. So often, I mentioned that I'd give anything to be in the House of Representatives. But I never dreamed it would come true." She pauses. "I went to law school, after the birth of my first child. And I worked at my law practice in between the births of my next two children. It wasn't easy," the Congresswoman recalls. "I even established my office near the elementary school, so I'd be available should the children need me. It was a struggle, but worth every minute of it! Then I got interested in politics," she says.

Representative Holt always had an interest in government, so she made her initial venture into local party politics. After graduation from the University of Florida Law School, she wanted to run for the state legislature. In her district, however, a woman would never be considered a serious candidate for a legislative office. Women could get administrative assignments in Anne Arundel County, but that's about all. Mrs. Holt reasoned that the men would be willing to accept a woman as a clerk, so she chose the position of clerk of the circuit court as a way of getting earnest recognition of her intentions to serve. As a practicing lawyer, she was aware of the needs of the county. Many of the laws and procedures of the court system were archaic.

"This was a good way to begin and make oneself known without making anyone angry. There was a job to be done . . . a hard one. But I was willing to assume this responsibility, if it would provide an entrée to the state legislature." Her district was composed of three times as many Democrats as Republicans, and her opponent was a well-known, entrenched Democrat. "It was a struggle—a woman and a Republican too—but I beat him! I guess . . . I got away with it, because no one else was willing to take the risk of running against him. But more important the victory gave me the opportunity to prove that I was capable," she concludes with a smile.

In 1972, she was elected to the 93rd Congress and has been re-elected two more times in landslide victories. In her first term, Congresswoman Holt was appointed to the House Armed Services Committee; in her second, to the House Budget Committee. This committee sets national spending priorities. Her role includes service on the National Security Task Force and the Budget Process Task Force within this important committee. On the Armed Services Committee, she has worked to eliminate military policies that discriminate against women. Mrs. Holt is a member of the Intelligence and Nuclear Energy Subcommittee and the Personnel Subcommittee of this committee.

In the seventh grade, when Congresswoman Holt set her goals on a seat in the House, she chose law as a beginning career for two reasons. First, law was the usual preparation for public service then. Second, she had to earn a living. But her youthful ambition would never have been realized without the strong support of a loving father. Mrs. Holt, the oldest child, was encouraged to follow her interests. "I remember my grandmother, whom I loved and respected very much and who had a tremendous influence on my life, saying, 'This is a very stupid thing to do. Why in the world are you wasting your time? You've got a very good husband and ought to just settle back and enjoy it. You're wasting your time going to school.' But, of course, that's what was expected of most girls then," she explains.

Naturally Congresswoman Holt doesn't take all the credit for her successes. She is happily married to Duncan M. Holt. "A super husband! He's very secure and without hangups. We have a sharing relationship. When necessary, he's taken his turn with the children, cooks the meals, or whatever." She beams happily. Their three children, Rachel, Edward, and Victoria, have observed the tremendous amount of personal involvement needed to become a successful politician. "And it may have turned them off . . . the sacrifices are so great. They are not considering political careers. There is so little time to spend together as a family and what little you have becomes very precious." She grows rather pensive. "That is why you have to guard your personal life very carefully. One of the reasons for the high attrition rates in marriages and relationships among congressional members is that they become so very involved. Their work becomes all-consuming. There is great danger in blocking out everything and everyone else. This job can become your reasons . . . for being, if you're not careful. And then it's really difficult for someone else who's not involved in it. A congressional wife who is not part of her husband's day-to-day activities leads a very lonely life. So one must make a strong effort to preserve that relationship. Personally, I would not want to be this involved if I had young children. Yet some of the congresswomen are doing it and doing it very well. For me, that part of my life, when I was raising my children, was very precious. Being close to them was most important to me, so I made them my first priority. The years pass so quickly, and you miss a great deal by not being with them. I am really proud of my family. They're all just wonderful." Congresswoman Holt's family now consists of three grandchildren also. Her eyes look toward the family pictures on her large desk. "It's so easy to return to political life—both for a man or a woman—so it's worth taking time out," she reasons softly.

Congresswoman Holt has had many legislative successes of which she is eager to talk. The Homestead Act—her amendment to the Housing Bill—is one of her greatest achievements. "This bill permitted the federal government to give homes back to private ownership through the one dollar purchase in the equity. A great concept, I think. It got HUD off dead-center and enabled them to release 80,000 homes to people who needed them. This example had national implications, and I accomplished it in my freshman term." She recalls another feat. "The service to my district is very important to me too. Our government is becoming so big and far removed from the people . . . so bureaucratic that it is impersonal. We spend a great deal of money here trying to provide for the needs of the nation, but the individual citizen back home doesn't know where or how to get services. It worries me. So I devote a tremendous amount of my time making sure that government does respond to people. I'm on the Budget Committee where I can have input. My legislative work is very important to me." Proof of this is a significant paperback edited by the Congresswoman. It is titled *The Case Against the Reckless Congress.* The book, published in 1976, covers a wide range of current policy issues written by members of Congress who specialize in those particular areas. The book serves to remind members of Congress of their responsibilities. The congresswoman's introduction includes this caution:

"In domestic policy, the fundamental issue is whether Americans will be ruled by a paternal, federal bureaucracy that offers benefits in return for submission to central planning and control of every significant aspect of their lives. Remember, social and economic planning by the central government is the surest road to tyranny, because a plan can be enforced only by the exercise of tyranny. The people are best served by policy set at the state and local levels. The cause of freedom is best served at a level where the individual voice can be heard."

It's a full life being a member of Congress. This member has very little free time. And what little she has is spent sleeping. She reveals this with a twinkle in her eyes. "Actually we have a lot of interests and one of them is sailing. We have a sailboat and sail on the Chesapeake Bay whenever possible. I like to garden and do handcrafts like needlepoint, too."

Congresswoman Holt sees women assuming roles of greater importance in politics in the near future. She recalls this example. "When I ran for Congress the first time and was elected, no woman was running for any office in Maryland. I was the first woman to be elected to Congress in a general election. One had followed her husband. But in the next election, thirteen women ran for local legislative jobs in my home county. They went around knocking on doors, and people were doubtful about voting for a woman. But people remembered their votes for Marjorie Holt who, they believed, was doing a good job. So they voted for the women. So we are seeing that kind of effect all over the country. As we become aware of our talents and people begin to recognize them, women will move forward. And now we have two more congresswomen from Maryland . . . the highest proportion in representation. It's really a snowballing effect. So hopefully we'll be in the Senate soon and even the presidency."

To the question about advising potential female politicians, she remarked, "The answer is involvement. I think the law is a wonderful profession for a woman. I'm very romantic about it. I really miss it. I love it and often think I'd really like to get back into practice. But there is no special kind of education that really prepares you. One must be involved in civic activities with your political party if possible and have a knowledge of what's happening in the community. People must get a chance to know you and observe your abilities. This is the groundwork! I remember going to all the women's groups to get their support a year previous to the election. This kind of organizational preparation is vital."

Mrs. Holt is a warm and receptive person with a sense of humor. Despite her achievements, she is unpretentious and modest. She talks about an incident which occurred when she was a freshman in Congress. "After winning with such fanfare, I really though I'd arrived . . . a famous congresswoman from Maryland. I was walking along the corridor with a noted congressman from Georgia whom I recognized. And I thought to myself—how wonderful to be acknowledged by him. After all there were so few congresswomen around, so I was sure he knew that I was Congresswoman Holt. We chatted amiably all the way to the elevator and entered together. Then, as he started to get out of the elevator, he turned and said, 'Now whose secretary are you?' " It was a deflating experience that she can view with humor today. Now nobody makes that kind of mistake, because Congresswoman Holt has made her mark and is recognized by everyone.

Margaret M. Heckler

When an important bill is being presented and debated in the House, everyone wants to go on record either in support of or in opposition to the issue. The constituents back home are concerned and interested in the way they are being represented. And every politician is aware of this responsibility. When the buzzer sounds throughout the halls, elevators, and offices, men and women come running from everywhere. That buzzer means that the voting is about to begin. So it was the day of my interview with Congresswoman Heckler.

The congresswoman's efficient secretary kept watching the clock as the 1:00 P.M. time drew nearer. Mrs. Heckler was in the House. A pay raise for the members of Congress was being debated. She felt that it was important for her to speak in opposition to it. By 1:15 P.M., it became apparent that Congresswoman Heckler would not have time to return to her office, so we would have to go to her.

We literally raced to the elevator which took us to the basement. Members of Congress, staff, aides, messengers, and tourists bumped shoulders in the foot race to the Capitol.

Subterranean tunnels lead from the Longworth, Cannon, and Rayburn office buildings to the Capitol. We arrived breathlessly at the Rayburn Room on the second floor of the famous building This ornately decorated, formal, reception room was being prepared for some affair to be held later in the day. Men were busy shifting about large, potted palms and baskets of pink carnations and white gladioli. Congresswoman Heckler came running in out of breath, and greeted me warmly. The noise of moving tables and chairs was disturbing, so we picked up our things and hurried toward the congresswomen's reading room. Several congresswomen were chatting in the sitting room, so we looked into the kitchen. The well-appointed, immaculate room was unoccupied, and had a door. We settled for this oasis of privacy.

Later we toured the lounge, and I saw a small sitting room tastefully decorated in period furniture. Hanging from the center of the ceiling was an enormous, multi-crystal, pendant chandelier. Congresswoman Heckler explained. "The story goes that the beautifully hand-crafted chandelier originally hung in a reception room in the White House. One day, President Calvin Coolidge asked to have the windows opened for a breath of fresh air. The soft breezes from the Potomac set the crystals tingling musically. But the president could not abide the noise. 'Please remove that noisy intruder from this room,' he ordered. And so this magnificent work of art hangs silently in the congresswomen's lounge." A rather large white, marble plaque hangs above a settee. The features on the plaque are those of John Quincy Adams, the sixth president of the United States. The inscription advises that this former president died in this room on February 23, 1848, and probably on this settee.

Congresswoman Heckler has that bouncing, energetic, good humor that is infectious. One feels relaxed with her immediately. A Republican from Massachusetts, she joined the 90th

Congress in 1967 and has been re-elected five times since then. Her interest in politics began while attending Albertus Magnus College in New Haven, Connecticut. She ran for an office called speaker of the house of student legislature of Connecticut. She campaigned on every college campus and was elected by an enormous plurality. Although she had expected to win, her real moment of triumph came when she turned the rostrum over to her opponent so he could preside for one hour. She went to relax in the lounge for an hour, but within ten minutes students were at the door begging her to return to the meeting. The chamber was in total disarray and the student legislature had broken into chaos. They asked that she return and restore order to the deliberations. "From that point on, I felt very adequate."

After graduation from Boston College Law School, Congresswoman Heckler worked as a volunteer for candidates running for office. She felt that the candidates were not effective in reaching the voters. "I felt that I could use my legal experience as a public service, so that's how I began," she concludes.

Congresswoman Heckler is married and has managed to fulfill the roles of wife, mother, and politician without any difficulty. "You see, when I ran for speaker in the student legislature, my husband-to-be, John Heckler, was my campaign manager. So we reached an understanding very early in our courting days that continued on through my law career of ten years. He's a very enlightened and liberated man. He supports me in my career and I support his career ambitions. And together, we place a great deal of emphasis on our three children's growth and development. I'm proud of them. The children have a sense of service to others and an understanding of human nature. I think they have a broadmindedness that's valuable to them as human beings and they're going to be good citizens."

In her first bid for elective office, Mrs. Heckler won a seat on the Massachusetts Governor's Council. She was the first woman to hold that post and was re-elected in 1964. Mrs. Heckler served until her election to Congress. In that primary, she challenged Joe Martin, former Speaker of the House and its minority leader. To the surprise of the Republican leadership, she beat Joe Martin in the primary and later won in the general election.

In the 95th Congress, Congresswoman Heckler holds coveted seats on the Joint Economic Committee, Agriculture Committee, Veterans' Affairs Committee, and the select House Committee on Ethics—the only woman on each committee. In her work on the committees and in the full House, she has been a leader in getting legislation passed in the areas of the economy, the environment, energy, consumer protection, senior citizens, personal privacy, education, child care, congressional ethics, and equal rights for women. Her activities in these and other areas have won her wide acclaim from progressive and reform-minded groups throughout the country. She serves on a total of eight subcommittees under the four committees mentioned earlier.

Congresswoman Heckler is proud of her work on the Equal Credit Opportunity Act. "I was the initial sponsor of the act. I served on the Banking Committee with Congressman Ed Koch of New York. He handled the Democratic side and I managed the Republicans, and we ultimately succeeded with this piece of legislation. It eventually passed and became law. Another fond success was my work on the ban against women in home mortgages. I authored that legislation, too, when I served on that committee. I created the position of Small Business Advocate through an amendment to the Small Business Act. I did this, because I'm very interested in not only having individuals break the barriers and survive, but also in having small businesses survive. They are the very key to the American economy!" she declares with passion.

Outgoing and vivacious with well-defined leadership skills, it is obvious to see why this congresswoman was selected as chairperson of the first delegation of congresswomen to go on a fact-finding mission to the People's Republic of China. The two-week mission was also the first congressional representation after President Ford's visit of December 2 to 5, 1975. A major purpose of the trip was to understand better the significant problems both internal and international that the Chinese believe they confront; to appraise the methods which the Chinese adopted for solving their problems and their likelihood of success; and to observe first-hand the links between domestic concerns and foreign policy intentions of the Chinese leadership.

Congresswoman Heckler's report of the congresswomen's visit relates some of the women's reactions. "Each member of the delegation reached individual conclusions with respect to major topics, both domestic and foreign. All of us have been making and will continue to make separate judgments and policy recommendations where appropriate. The trip, although brief, was intense in its effect. Each congresswoman brought individual interests, assumptions, experiences, and expertise to a country that most had not visited before. Circumstances limited our ability to see much of such a highly diverse and varied nation, but our experience was sufficient to make us realize the very considerable diversity in customs, habits, style, and perhaps goals that characterize the People's Republic of China."

Members of the delegation included Representatives Patsy T. Mink, Bella S. Abzug, Yvonne B. Burke, Elizabeth Holtzman, Patricia Schroeder, Corrine C. Boggs, Cardiss Collins, Millicent Fenwick, Helen S. Meyner, and Gladys Noon Spellman. The group visited China from December 30, 1975 to January 9, 1976.

Mrs. Heckler sees women continuing to make gains, with more impressive numbers making their breakthrough at the grass roots level. Although women will reach the pinnacle— the presidency—one day, that day is a long way off. It's a very difficult adjustment for a person to come and live in Washington. A career woman or a bachelor can do it without too many major family problems. "In my case, my husband is in the investment business which had a Washington branch. He initially intended to come to Washington, but I won my first congressional seat by a narrow margin and, had he gained a Washington office, it would have meant a loss of his Boston clients. Besides, I didn't think it was fair for him to give up his career. So I brought the children to Washington with me. My oldest, Belinda, is now a sophomore at Dartmouth College. I have a high school senior, Alison, and I have a son, John, Jr. We worked it out well, because we concentrated on making it work."

Congresswoman Heckler continues. "Women's greatest recognition will come when the country elects its first female vice–president. The public will realize that a woman can be proficient in making decisions for the country, and then we'll have a woman president. But I don't see that happening in this decade, however."

People are this congresswoman's avocation. She derives great pleasure from going to the local districts, speaking to groups of factory workers, senior citizens, shoppers, and passersby in the streets. Beyond that, her main enjoyment comes from her family. Dancing, music, and theater are other interests, when there is time. She gives and attends small dinner parties where friends can discuss issues informally. "Friendships mean a great deal to me," she reveals.

"The very first day I came to Congress," she recalls, "I had a funny, but sad, experience. I was considerably younger than other congresswomen. And I heard a congressman whisper to a colleague, 'How did that secretary get on the floor of Congress?' I was a duly elected member, but he wasn't ready for change, obviously."

Congresswoman Heckler has presented a strong, positive model for her children. Early in her career, when she ran for the Governor's Council in Massachusetts, she remembers this conversation at the breakfast table with her three children. They were four, six, and eight years of age at the time. "When I grow up, I'm going to a governor like Mommy," John Jr., the youngest declared. But Alison, the six-year-old, cried, "Oh you can't be a governor—you're a boy!" John and Margaret Heckler have instilled a sense of individual worth in their children and a belief that one should aspire to whatever heights one's talents can be best expressed. "I should like for one of my children to go into politics and public office. I feel very privileged to have been chosen to serve the people." Pride and humility intermingled in Congresswoman Heckler's voice and on her face.

Elizabeth Holtzman

If you've ever wondered about what takes place in the district office of a member of the United States Congress, just spend a couple of hours in the storefront quarters of Congresswoman Elizabeth Holtzman. Affectionately called Liz by almost everyone, she is surrounded by a devoted staff of varying ages and ethnic bacgrounds who help her serve the needs of the community. The anxious voice on the telephone is calmed and reassured by a counselor familiar with the caller's problem. A man without an appointment worries about his rent. It was paid with a now worthless money order. He was even in the wrong district office, but one of Liz's young aides helped him anyway. Two young men squirmed on hard, straight-backed chairs. Their acne-spotted, scrubbed faces, recent haircuts, and neatly pressed clothing were part of the look they hoped would impress the congresswoman. Both wanted recommendations to service academies. An elderly woman waited patiently to hear about her social security check.

The telephone rang continuously with requests for transportation to a hospital for a handicapped woman, heat for a cold apartment, a delayed Medicare reimbursement payment, and a variety of major and minor crises. All of these received the prompt attention of one of the congresswoman's obviously competent, cheerful assistants. Their enthusiasm was as infectious as their smiles. Jan, as appointment secretary, remarked that most days began this way. I then wondered how Liz Holtzman began this provocative career.

Miss Holtzman is the product of a well-ordered, middle class home and community in the Flatbush section of Brooklyn, New York. After graduation from Abraham Lincoln High School, she attended Radcliffe College where she earned a B.A. degree with honors and graduated magna cum laude. Liz made history by being the first Lincoln graduate to attend Radcliffe. In 1962, she entered Harvard Law School where she received her J.D. degree in 1965. At Harvard, Miss Holtzman became one of the founders of the Law Students' Civil Rights Research Council, a nationwide law students' organization. One summer, while still a student, she worked on civil rights cases in Georgia. The following year, in addition to her legal studies, she taught English at Harvard College. Miss Holtzman was a good student, and a promising law career seemed inevitable.

Her career as an attorney began and developed with experience in two prestigious law firms in New York. After two years of law practice, she was asked to join Mayor John Lindsay's staff at City Hall. "I thought it sounded interesting. And since I hadn't worked in his campaign, the invitation was really unexpected—right out of the blue," Congresswoman Holtzman explains. "But I had no aspirations for public office at all—none at all, then." She was appointed an assistant to Mayor Lindsay with special responsibility for parks, recreation and cultural affairs. Her successes included the installation of fifteen mini-pools and additional safety matting for playgrounds. She worked to expand the hours and services of museums and libraries, too.

Working on complex, urban problems appealed to her. "I discovered governmental work could be challenging, exciting, and interesting. I got more involved and saw an opportunity to do things that would really help New York City. I felt deeply about that. . . ." She pauses. "Up until that time, I'd always considered politics as sort of a dirty word, smoky back-rooms, double-dealing sort of thing. I believed all of this was an intrinsic part of politics," the congresswoman reveals. "Then I looked around me and saw the elected officials crowded around City Hall. And I thought if they can get elected to public office, why can't I?"

She began by running for state committeewoman as a reform Democrat in the Flatbush section of Brooklyn in June 1971. Miss Holtzman resided in the 16th Congressional District—Emanuel Celler's district, but she had never received a newsletter from him. Nor did anyone ever mention his name. It was apparent that he was not doing the job in Washington that needed to be done for the district. But Emanuel Celler had become sort of an institution in Congress. He no longer bothered to campaign, because his re-election was a certainty. He had held office for twenty-five terms. Miss Holtzman's announcement to oppose Celler in 1972 was no threat to him. Celler dismissed her challenge. But she toppled him by winning the primary by a scant 611 votes. She scored an easy victory in the November election and became a national figure by being the youngest woman ever sent to the House.

Congresswoman Holtzman gave up her law practice when she went to Washington. She kept her pledge to be a full-time public servant and work only for her constituents. The congresswoman's family and friends supported her ambitions enthusiastically, believing, like her, that a woman can do any job as well as a man. A review of some of her activities over the past four years is ample proof of this. On the budget committee, she has worked to increase spending on human needs, cut unnecessary defense expenditures, eliminate waste, and close tax loopholes. She attacked inadequate Medicare reimbursement. At her request, the General Accounting Office (Congress' watchdog agency) studied why New York's elderly were not receiving proper reimbursement from Medicare for doctors' bills. She was successful in gaining increases in supplemental social security income payments for 84,000 New Yorkers.

She joined with others in introducing legislation to remove permanently the federal means test requirement for senior citizen centers. Her amendment adding $138 million to help states and localities fight crime was passed by the House in June 1976. Congresswoman Holtzman chaired a House Budget Committee hearing on the impact of a New York City default that produced key facts and figures which helped obtain federal aid for New York City. The Holtzman subway safety amendment, which was enacted as part of the Urban Mass Transit Act of 1973, empowers the secretary of transportation to hold up federal funds if any transit authority does not remedy unsafe subway conditions.

During the year of 1975 alone, seventeen Holtzman amendments were added to the new Rules of Criminal Procedure for the Federal Courts. The congresswoman also introduced bills in February 1976 and January 1977 to bar irrelevant questioning about a rape victim's prior sexual conduct.

Congresswoman Holtzman's name is a very familiar one in the 16th Congressional District. She keeps her constituents informed through her *Reports From Washington* newsletter. In addition to major successes like blocking the move of the Navy Resale Systems, saving 800 jobs, she attends to the needs of local residents—the grassroots of any community. These are some examples:

She obtained a neighborhood New York Telephone Company payment center for the convenience of residents who formerly had to travel distances to pay their bills.

City dwellers know how dangerous potholes are to automobiles and pedestrians alike. Congresswoman Holtzman's efforts got many repaired.

Deserted buildings attract undesirables like drifters or even packs of stray dogs. The congresswoman got several of these buildings boarded up for the protection of residents.

Abandoned cars left in driveways can interfere with vitally needed services of police, ambulances, and fire engines—in addition to normal access to the streets for tenants. Liz Holtzman had 12 such cars removed.

Senior citizens and families like to enjoy the parks, but broken tables and benches can be a hazard. She had them removed.

Ocean Parkway, a broad multi-laned and tree-lined roadway, runs through the heart of her district. Residents would like to preserve its beauty, but repaving and reconstruction attempts got bogged down in bureaucratic handling. Miss Holtzman was able to cut through all the necessary steps and get the work started. The parkway and mall are being rebuilt according to the wishes of the community.

The list is endless but includes repair of street lights, cleaning of catch-basins, installation of warning traffic signals, and replacement of a sewer cover. All of these are very important services to constituents.

Congresswoman Holtzman opened the first congressional district office in her district in fifty years.

Miss Holtzman is asked what particular personal characteristic has helped her to become so successful. She laughed softly and blushed slightly. "Well. It's very hard to say. Initially I guess my will power or pluck, since most people didn't think winning the race was possible. But I think part of my success comes from not being daunted as other people are by conventional wisdom. I assess the possibilities and ask what can be done. And I think being willing to take chances and not being always constrained by thoughts of money or fame have been important."

Unlike some of her colleagues, Congresswoman Holtzman does not see women playing a particular or specific role in any area of public life. "When I was practicing law, women lawyers were doing everything from advising corporations on corporate mergers, to determining tax consequences in various transactions, to going to court and litigating in trials. And I've met many women since then who are stockbrokers, competent scientists, and other skilled professionals." She leans forward eagerly. "The only thing that really hampers women from participating as fully as they can in accord with their talents is the inhibition that society has instilled in them as to what is appropriate. And of course, the discrimination from men is ever present," Liz states emphatically. "But I think it's very important for young women to realize the road is really open now. And they should try to follow their own instincts, interests, and talents, and make the most of them. A career in politics can be rewarding and challenging and not corrupting—just as a career in physics, mathematics, or high finance. Anything and everything should be open to them. They should pursue whatever they want to do."

During the last two congressional sessions, there have been several things which she found rewarding. "One was, of course, my participation in the House Judiciary Committee's impeachment inquiries." Elizabeth Holtzman participated in the committee's deliberations on the impeachment of former

President Nixon. Her astute and brilliant questioning brought her instant fame and the respect of millions of viewers. She appears very serious and the tone of her voice is solemn. "The second was my questioning of President Gerald Ford about the pardon issued by him to former President Nixon. It turned out that I was the only one that had the courage to ask him the questions that were really on everyone's mind." She relaxes somewhat and continues. "The third is raising the issue of the failure of the Immigration Service to go after more than sixty Nazi war criminals in this country. After pressuring them for more than three years, they finally took concrete steps to seek out and deport these criminals. The fourth was my amendment to the social security insurance program which provided increased benefits for poverty-stricken aged, blind, and disabled recipients in New York, California, Massachusetts, Wisconsin, and Nevada. Emergency check replacements along with these benefits made a significant difference in the lives of these poor people." Throughout the interview, her posture has been low-key, positive, and self-assured. She speaks with confidence and a certain amount of partially restrained fervor.

Some young women considering careers in public life are concerned about what they see as an almost impossible contradiction in roles. They are puzzled by the dilemma of postponing marriage and children for a career. Miss Holtzman's reply to this possible problem is straightforward. "Well, any woman who's going to have a career and a family must be well organized. And she must learn how to budget her time. I've had good examples in my own family. My mother is a college professor of languages. She taught, wrote, and raised me and my brother. I would say that she did a good job. I turned out all right and my twin brother is a neurosurgeon. So it's never seemed inconsistent to me to have a family and pursue one's interests outside of the home. The women members of Congress learn how to manage. I think the more interesting question is that we as a society are concerned deeply about how women relate to their children, but we don't have any of the same expectations about men. I would hope that when the question of women's rights in this country becomes more fully understood that we'll also be concerned about the stereotypes regarding men's relationships to their families. We should rethink these stereotypes. Perhaps it's not good for either parent to be working late at night or away for long hours.

"If she has a career, a woman has to make the same choices as a man," the congresswoman continues. "The important thing in a marriage or any relationship is that people respect each other. And one partner should not think that whatever he or she is doing is the more important job. This would be a very destructive relationship to have. Respect and understanding without domination of either person is positive and healthy."

Miss Holtzman was a literature and history major at Radcliffe. So she doesn't recommend any particular area of concentration in college for a budding politician. But she does advise a program that is well planned and offers a variety of experience. In other words, a good education is essential. "Learn how to read carefully, question things, take a lively interest in what's happening, and think analytically. Law school was important for me, because, when I ran for Congress the first time, it made people realize that I was a serious kind of person. I mean a serious contender. Perhaps it may still be true that women will not be taken seriously in election to public office unless they are lawyers. I don't think a law background is necessary for a man or a woman who wants to hold public office. But there are certain benefits in some areas and a knowledge of law is helpful. Although it isn't necessary in order to do the work, it still may be helpful for a woman to be a lawyer . . . so she can say to the public 'I do have the credentials.' "

A congresswoman has a demanding and full schedule. Moments of relaxation are rare. "I relax in lots of ways. I like to listen to operas. I like Mozart operas the best. But I enjoy the works of Verdi and Wagner. I like music a great deal. I guess my tastes are eclectic. Travel is another one of my interests. I have been fortunate enough to have traveled many places around the world. It has always taught me a great deal about how much people have in common. And, at the same time, how much separates us, unfortunately. But I try not to do it on the government's payroll unless it is absolutely related to the work of Congress. I've been very careful about that."

Miss Holtzman is optimistic about the future roles of women in public office. She forsees the day when cabinet-level positions will be the rule of the day. "One thing puzzles me about recent nominations to high-level positions for women. But, of course, I was not close to the process by which President Carter selected the Cabinet. I was puzzled by his statement that he couldn't find many highly qualified women. Just in my brief experience in Congress, I have come in contact with a number of women who are extremely capable, intelligent, practical, well organized, and who have good judgment; women whom you could easily admire as really good and definitely talented people. I'm disappointed that he made such statements. I think there's a large number of well-qualified women. Most of the women who've made their way to high positions in government, business, education, or the like, are, generally speaking, rather extraordinary people because they've had to surmount discrimination. Most of them are more capable than their male counterparts in all of these positions. They're much more unusual and much more talented. I would hope that one of the things that this administration can do is to bring many more women into public life." She thinks for a moment. "Maybe the scope of the search committee was not broad enough, because the women are out there."

From all indications, congressmen appear to be taking congresswomen more seriously these days. Congresswoman Holtzman agrees. "One incident that changed the image of women for congressmen was the appointment of Congresswoman Jordan and myself to the House Judiciary Committee. We were the first women to serve on that committee. During the televised impeachment debate, we didn't embarrass anyone and performed quite effectively," she states simply.

The congresswoman enjoys what she's doing and, although people have urged her to consider higher office, she plans to remain a representative for the present. "The thing that's been most exciting about all of this is that it was so unpredictable. Three years before I ran for Congress, if anyone had asked me if I planned to become a congresswoman, I would have just laughed. I would hope more young women would be given the encouragement to consider politics as a serious career possibility. We really need the talents and contributions of honest, dedicated, and competent people. The temptation to be corrupt is no greater there than in any other kind of occupation. It is possible to preserve one's sense of integrity and politics is a very exciting kind of life."

Liz appears less tense now. She offers these thoughts. "I think one of the most flattering things that happened to me occurred right after I won the primary against Mr. Celler. A number of young women who helped in my campaign said, 'Well, Liz . . . I'm going to go to law school and beat you.' Of course, they were joking. But the important thing was that they were now aware of new possibilities and new horizons. Their eyes had been opened. And this was very heartening."

She clasps her hands and laughs. "I hope they don't run against me, of course."

Unlike certain groups, like the Black Caucus, congress-women do not vote as a block. They are separated by party differences and ideological differences, so it may never be possible to get them together as a group. "I see women as being individualistic in their thinking and performances. However, we do work together. For example, Congresswoman Chisholm's district adjoins mine. We have developed a good working relationship. Even though our constituents have different needs, at times, we face similar local problems. I have great respect for her and have learned a great deal from her." She shifts her position. "I hope women office-holders can learn to work together and share power so that they can accomplish things as a group. It would be a waste if they followed the same pattern that has been so prevalent in politics of the past . . . just ego politics. That's one of the things I hope doesn't happen to women."

Women don't have to resort to femininity to get attention, according to the congresswoman. "Some may think they have to, but that's their problem." The precise, sharp delivery is almost in contrast to the warm, good natured disposition of this young woman of great promise. She is quietly and politely friendly, but she is also a very private person. Liz Holtzman is definitely a woman on the move and her impact will be felt far beyond the boundaries of the 16th Congressional District of Brooklyn.

Barbara Jordan

Some call it fate. Others say it's timing—being in the right place at the right time. Many regard it as chance or luck. But whatever it is, it happens to a very, few select people—and Barbara Charlene Jordan is one.

Almost unknown, except in Texas, she burst upon the national scene and into everyone's home through the magic of television. Miss Jordan, a member of the House Judiciary Committee, sat listening intently to the debate. The debate on whether to recommend the impeachment of President Richard M. Nixon was into its second day. Suddenly we heard Chairman Rodino's rasping voice roar, "The chair recognizes . . . the gentlelady from Texas." Our eyes focused on a bright orange dress, a somewhat heavy figure and a full, round, but attractive, black face. But it was the voice that immobilized us. Clear, precise, sharp, and resonant. She spoke to all of us and yet to each of us. " 'We, the people'—it is a very eloquent beginning. But when the Constitution of the United States was completed on the 17th of September in 1787, I was not included in that 'We, the people.' I felt for many years that somehow George Washington and Alexander Hamilton just left me out by mistake. But through the process of amendment, interpretation, and court decision I have finally been included in 'We, the people. . . .' " The gentlelady from Texas would go down in history . . . the date was July 25, 1974.

Barbara Jordan was born in Houston, Texas, on February 21, 1936, to Benjamin and Arlyne Jordan. The daughter of a Baptist minister who was also a warehouse clerk, Miss Jordan grew up poor but ambitious. Her father stressed achievement. "I never intended," she recalls, "to be a run-of-the-mill person." The Jordan family, including her two older sisters, Bennie and Rose Mary, lived in heavily populated Harris County. Equipped with an extraordinary intellect, determination, and parents who encouraged and supported her efforts to use these gifts, she decided to attend college after graduation from Houston's public schools. For a short while, she considered becoming a chemist or a pharmacist. But she finally decided on a law career. She told one interviewer that she did not know anyone "who ever heard of an outstanding pharmacist." Mr. Jordan worked hard and provided each of his daughters with a college education.

At Texas Southern University, an all-black school, Miss Jordan was a debating champion. She graduated magna cum laude in 1956 with a major in political science. When asked about her perfect diction and precise delivery, she explains. "My father's great loves were his family, his faith, and his language. He would be critical when my report card would have one B intermingled with all the As. It is from him that I learned the precise diction."

Miss Jordan may be credited with many firsts. Her admission to Boston University Law School in 1956 is just one example. She was the first female of minority status to enter the elite institution. After graduation, she returned to Houston. But during the early sixties, even an impressive law degree didn't mean that a black woman could overturn tradition in Houston. She returned to her parents' home and set up a law practice on the dining-room table.

After practicing law for three years, Miss Jordan decided to try for elective office. She had to borrow the $500 filing fee. She remembers, "I rarely saw my opponent in person, but was confronted by his face on many billboards and on the television screen. He was obviously well financed." Miss Jordan thought naively that if she worked hard, people would disregard race, sex, and poverty and elect her. When she lost, Miss Jordan tried to console herself with the fact that she had received 46,000 votes to her opponent's 65,000. However, she had to admit finally that her opponent's edge was money, power, and influence. She discovered, like other female congressional members, that frequently the candidate's qualifications are not a major factor. "It was clear that if I was to win the right to represent some of the people of Texas, I had to persuade the moneyed and politically influential interests either to support me or to remain neutral," she recalls.

Undaunted, Miss Jordan made a second bid for the Texas House of Representatives. She lost again, but by a smaller margin. "This time there was identifiable support in traditionally white, conservative precincts."

Although her supporters were encouraged by her showing, Miss Jordan was dismayed. However, she did serve as administrative assistant to the county judge of Harris County. For a while, she considered abandoning her dream of a political career in Texas and moving elsewhere. A 1966, reapportionment in the Senate helped to change her mind. Her new district was 38 percent black and 62 percent Chicanos and whites. The district also included many blue-collar workers.

This time Miss Jordan was not to be denied. She was elected to the Senate by a margin of two to one—the first black person of either sex to be elected to that exclusive body since 1883.

"To be effective, I had to get inside the club, not just inside the chamber," she explains. "I singled out the most influential and powerful members and was determined to gain their respect." Ever mindful of her responsibilities to her constituents, this articulate reformer applied her talents diligently to the task. Miss Jordan served on almost every Senate committee, chaired several of them, and built up a long record of achievements. These included legislation establishing the Texas Fair Employment Practices Commission, an improved workmen's compensation act, and the state's first minimum wage law. Miss Jordan won another first, too. She was named Senate president pro-tem. On June 10, 1972, in the traditional "Governor for a Day" ceremonies, she became the first black woman governor in the history of the United States.

By 1970, Miss Jordan's superb execution of intellect and judgment had won the attention and respect of the most powerful Texan of all—Lyndon Baines Johnson. The former president helped her get elected to the United States Congress in 1972. During the heated campaign, Miss Jordan avoided attacking the character of her opponent and stayed with the issues. Her quiet dignity gained her more than four times as many votes as her opponents. The primary victory intensified Miss Jordan's determination to work even harder in the general election.

Congresswoman Jordan came to Washington on January 3, 1973. Her experience in the Texas Senate made her acutely aware of the magnitude and range of power . . . like a spider with radiating spokes or arms. With power, one could reach indefinite heights doing good or evil. Miss Jordan joined the Congressional Black Caucus, but she wanted an assignment to the Judiciary Committee. "This committee dealt with the issues I was interested in," she comments. "All civil rights legislation, questions regarding the administration of justice, constitutional amendments are handled by the Judiciary Committee. I wanted to be on it." Former President Johnson helped her get the assignment. At the time, she had no idea that the committee would be involved with such matters as the confifirmation of a vice–president (the nomination of Gerald R. Ford to replace Spiro T. Agnew) and the impeachment of President Richard M. Nixon.

In an interview, the freshman congresswoman revealed her feelings. "I still could not take in that it was really going to happen. I have the same high regard for the officc of the president as the majority of Americans. He is a figure who towers above all other figures in the world. Certainly no one could seriously consider forcing the president to leave office before his term expired. This feeling stayed with me for a long time." The evidence that there had been criminal acts was overwhelming and President Nixon resigned. Congresswoman Jordan feels a deep commitment to the millions of minority people who are without a voice or political clout. "The long-range hope I have for this country is that it will grow stronger and that everybody can feel that they're in it, that it really does belong to us. There are many of my constituents who are black and poor who still do not feel that this country belongs to them, that the deal they have gotten is sour. They feel they are just going to live every day the best they can until they live no longer. I want to see the day when we—everybody can feel like we belong here, that this country has to survive because we have to survive, that our future is bound up in the future of the nation. I'd like to see that happen."

In her first term, the congresswoman introduced and sponsored many bills. Among the measures enacted are bills to:

- establish immediate cost of living increases for social security recipients
- establish a National Center on Child Development and Abuse
- prevent the destruction of the Office of Economic Opportunity
- amend the Safe Streets Act of 1968 to improve law enforcement and criminal justice
- authorize establishment of the Big Thicket National Biological Reserve in the State of Texas
- eliminate certain limitations on the use of federal funds for social service programs
- provide for programs of public service employment for the unemployed
- require congressional authorization for reinvolvement in Indochina
- continue twelve health programs scheduled for abolishment
- allocate water pollution control funds among states on a more equitable basis

When Congresswoman Jordan announced her intentions to seek re-election, she said, "I will continue my commitment to the responsive representation of the half million people of the 18th Congressional District of Texas and do what I can as a member of congress to enhance the quality of their lives."

Through her *Reports To The People*, Congresswoman Jordan keeps the voters of the 18th District informed of important legislation which affects them. In February 1976, she wrote of the Subcommittee on Intergovernmental Relations of the

House Government Operation Committee plan to shape a new general revenue sharing bill. The new bill would possibly contain these provisions: allow the city of Houston to count water and sewer fees as taxes—thus increasing its share of the formula; strengthen the rights Houstonians can exercise to determine how revenue sharing is spent by the city; and prescribe new procedures to make sure the money is not spent with a discriminatory purpose or effect. Her *Report* also told them of the Subcommittee on Monopolies and Commercial Law of the House Judiciary Committee intention to decide the future course of the investigation into the alleged monopolistic structure and practices of the oil industry. Another time, she alerted Houston voters to their new rape center, one of the few metropolitan areas in the country equipped to deal comprehensively with the crime of rape and its victims.

In addition to her membership on the House Committee on the Judiciary, Congresswoman Jordan serves on the House Committee on Government Operations and the Steering and Policy Committee of the House Democratic Caucus. Her major legislative achievements enacted into law include an amendment to the Voting Rights Act which expanded the coverage and provided for the printing of bilingual ballots. This modification overcame some of the voting barriers for Spanish-speaking and Indian citizens. Another is the repeal of federal authorization for state "Fair Trade" Laws which sanctioned vertical price fixing schemes. Manufacturers can no longer fix retail prices for their products. Detailed mandatory civil rights enforcement procedures for the Law Enforcement Assistance Administration and the Office of Revenue Sharing is also one of her successes.

Congresswoman Jordan's advocacy for research in health and education is reflected in her announcement on March 31, 1976 of a substantial grant to the University of Texas. The

$2 million award by the National Cancer Institute is in the form of a five-year training grant. Miss Jordan explained, "These federal funds will support advanced training in clinical cancer research for physicians who already have received broad credit in their specialty areas. Their training will enable them to leave Anderson Hospital to carry out their own cancer work, and they will be the leading scientists of the next generation."

This extremely active congresswoman has been named Democratic Woman of the Year by the Women's National Democratic Club and the *Ladies Home Journal* picked her as the 1975 Woman of the Year, too. In a poll by *Redbook Magazine*, Miss Jordan was selected as top "Woman who Could be President." She was a keynote speaker at the 1976 Democratic National Convention in New York City. B. J., as she is known to her staff, is a shrewd political figure.

Although she projects a very formal and formidable image, Miss Jordan is known to have her moments. She tends to prefer tailored clothing and minimal make-up. She's almost a workaholic and can be found in her office by nine o'clock every morning. She spends every afternoon on the House floor. After a twelve-to-fourteen hour day, she returns to her apartment in southwest Washington to study and prepare herself for the next day. Away from her office and congressional duties, she can relax and enjoy herself. With family and friends, Miss Jordan sings folk and soul music. It is said that the popular group "Gladys and Her Pips" is her favorite. Those who are fortunate enough to enjoy her company speak of her easy laugh and sharp wit.

The congresswoman's membership in professional organizations include the State Bar of Texas, the Massachusetts Bar, American Bar Association, and the Texas Trial Lawyers Association. She maintains membership in the NAACP and the Good Hope Baptist Church of Houston.

Congresswoman Jordan's demonstrated oratorical talent, keen perceptiveness, and impressive record in Congress had many people proposing her for higher office. The Black Caucus wanted to nominate her for vice–president of the United States, after her electrifying keynote address at the National Democratic Convention in 1976. Congresswoman Jordan rejected all efforts by this group to nominate her. Although she is a member of the caucus, the relationship is not close. "I'm neither a black politician, nor a woman politician—I am just a politician, a professional politician," she said in an interview. However, she interpreted the move as a desire to demonstrate in a symbolic way the concerns of black Americans and women. The press reported some time later that her real interest was the position of attorney general. But President Jimmy Carter did not extend an offer, so she remains in the Congress.

Congresswoman Jordan has not been an idle spectator. Her performance has motivated and inspired minority women, especially, to extend their hopes and aspirations toward greater self-fulfillment. As a role model, her success says, "You too can get a slice of the pie!"

Martha Keys

Congresswoman Keys is serving her second term as Representative of the 2nd District of Kansas. Born in Hutchinson, Kansas, in 1930, she is the first Kansan to serve on the Ways and Means Committee since 1946, and is the only female member. Appointment to this influential committee when only a freshman is quite an honor. She also serves on two subcommittees: the Subcommittee on Health and the Subcommittee on Unemployment Compensation.

Mrs. Keys began her political life more than fifteen years before she considered the candidacy of representative. She began by working for change in her own community. She increased her involvement, but her interests peaked when she worked on an open housing committee in New Jersey during the early sixties. Her concern was an effort to get laws which would effect open housing. Work on nonpartisan community activities—developing such things as arts councils, recrea-

119

tional facilities, and charity drives—was also part of her volunteer service.

Later she devoted her energies to partisan politics by working with and for political candidates. She also became involved with political activities like delegate procedural rules. She held a number of offices in her local Democratic party and served as the Kansan coordinator for the 1972 Democratic presidential campaign.

Congresswoman Keys received her bachelor's degree from the University of Kansas City. Her major was music. "I'm not a lawyer, so knowledge of the law is not essential for success. In fact, the most important qualification for a political career is the ability to work with people and accomplish change," she declares. Like most members of Congress, Mrs. Keys tries to alleviate local district problems through her work on committees. She also keeps her supporters informed of important legislation. In her *News from Martha Keys*, she wrote in August 1976 about the impact of the estate tax reform bill as follows: "It is important to make note of this legislation, because it provides much needed relief to small family farms and closely held family business. It contains a number of provisions which affect many Second District citizens. The legislation outlines a tax credit which updates the present unrealistic and outdated exemption set in 1942. It provides for a more equitable way of giving everyone the same amount of relief. A change in the marital deduction and recognition of joint tenancy will permit spouses to have part interest in the estate."

Congresswoman Keys is extremely active. The 95th Congress has been in session less than a month, and she has already introduced this legislation:

H.J. Res. 130   Resolution to amend the Constitution

of the United States to provide for balanced budgets and elimination of the federal indebtedness

H.R. 86 Legislation to require authorization of new budget authority for government programs at least every five years and to establish zero base budgeting

H.R. 115 To end discrimination in employment

H.R. 1502 To establish a solar energy loan administration

H.R. 1924 To provide that pay increases for members of Congress do not become effective until after the term in which it is approved

H.R. 139 To disapprove the proposed exemption of motor gasoline from the petroleum price regulations

H.J. 77 An amendment to the Constitution to provide for a single six year term for the president and six consecutive terms for members of the House of Representatives

H.R. 947 To require candidates for federal offices and Congress to file statements with United States controller general regarding income and financial matters

Other new bills To increase social security earnings' limitation to $4,800

To insure the participation of professional registered nurses in professional standards review organizations at all levels

The recommendation to increase the salaries of members of Congress was rejected by Mrs. Keys and all of the other congresswomen. She based her objection on the following facts: first, members of Congress receive compensation that is comparable to salary increases for other occupational categories' cost of living increases; secondly, able and capable people can be attracted to government service at present salary levels; and, third, the new administration has been able to attract cabinet-level talent at salaries for less than those available to them in the private sector. Despite the debates both pro and con, congressional members did get a pay raise. Because of laws enacted under former President Ford, no specific House vote was needed for the pay raise. Many members of Congress were not happy with the outcome. They will now try to pass legislation which will require full disclosure of income from all sources and limitations of private work. These limitations will help members give the citizens their "money's worth."

Congresswoman Keys speaks modestly of her many accomplishments, but the depth of her commitment is communicated by her direct approach and ready answers to any questions. Her expertise probably derives from her direct association in the political field with family members. She has worked with her brother-in-law, now Senator Gary Hart, as campaign manager. She served as Kansas coordinator for the McGovern for President effort. In keeping with the tradition of political families, she married Representative Andy Jacobs of Indiana, during her first term in office.

When she has a few moments, she and her husband just relax and do nothing. "Of course, we have that opportunity rarely. Music was my college major and the piano my particular outlet. It is very relaxing and enjoyable for me to play the piano. There's not much time for this anymore either. I enjoy the outdoors and love to take long walks. I'm not an active sports enthusiast, probably because I have no sports skills. But I love exercise and being out of doors," the congresswoman reveals with a wide smile.

The roles of wife, mother, and political figure are not contradictory for Mrs. Keys. Perhaps one reason is that her children were not very young when she came to Washington. "I have two sons and two daughters—Carol, 26, Bryan, 24, Dana, 20, and Scott, 16," she says with a mother's pride. After a short pause, she continues. "Scott, of course, attends high school here in Washington. Bryan is also here doing an architectural internship," she adds.

"During the young and formative years, I made my children my first responsibility. So I had no problems in roles. None at all! I stayed home with them. This was my own personal choice. But it is not necessary to stay home to exercise that responsibility well. But that's the way I preferred, when they were young." Her tone is not defensive. She speaks openly and directly when expressing her feelings.

When asked about her favorite piece of legislation, she replies. "I'm very proud of the child care credits which was my amendment on the Ways and Means Committee. This was part of the tax reform bill last year. It meant that more than 2,000,000 working parents or single parents with the responsibility of minor children could get that recognition of that very, very necessary expense in order to enable them to work. Before that time, it had been a very limited deduction available to people of lower incomes and to young parents who hadn't bought a home yet and therefore didn't itemize or use the long form for declaring income."

Congresswoman Keys is very optimistic about the future role of women in our government. "There'll be a woman vice–president and a viable female candidate for president long before I die. I'm very definite about that," she exclaims with enthusiasm.

Her advice to young women who might seek careers in political life is unique. "I think that one of the most important points is this. It's an interesting thing, at this time at least, most of the women who are in public office . . . at the level of Congress . . . are not women who thought of it as a career when they were younger. The very nature of our society has not allowed that to this time And I think that is one of their strongest points. To them, it is not an all-consuming thing. As women are able, at this point in our societal evolution, to think about wanting to become politicians or assume a policy-making role and to plan ahead at an early age is most exciting. It's most important that they really keep sight of their goals and motivation . . . the true ones of serving some political interest of change. Otherwise we might see women lose what they have now. I mean that unique willingness to stand up for certain things, vote for certain issues without regard for the next election. Young women should contemplate and plan ahead for careers in public life. We need them! But I trust and hope that they never lose sight of the real motivation for public service. It isn't money or prestige or the next rung on the ladder. But it is hoping to accomplish the kind of change that will make lives . . . American lives . . . wherever they live—be it in the country side, urban or inner city, sub-urban or whatever—more rewarding and full."

She pauses to catch her breath. "It seems to me that's what we need here now. Women, percentage-wise, seem to be less corrupted by the goals of individual and commercial gain which tend to cause people to lose sight of their real mission." Congresswoman Keys ends on a very thoughtful note. Her motto is clear—service and dedication with minimal thought to personal ambition or gain. The telephone rings, and she is advised that her presence is needed for a quorum to continue the imporant business of the Ways and Means Committee. She gathers her notes quickly and waves a friendly goodby as she hurries down the long corridor to the elevators.

Marilyn Lloyd

Although it was midweek and important congressional issues were being discussed on the floor, Congresswoman Lloyd was taking a few moments out to prepare a forty-five second tape for local television and radio airing to her constituents in Tennessee. She is in Washington, but the folks back home would know her views. The tape concerned a local issue of great significance to the people of the 3rd District of Tennessee.

As a former small business owner, she and her late husband, Mort, owned and operated radio station WTTI in Dalton, Georgia for six years. He was also a television newscaster. They owned an agricultural flight service in Winchester, Tennessee, too. The Lloyds sold their business interests to pursue their political ambitions.

Congresswoman Lloyd has been active in politics many years. She campaigned and worked beside her late husband in all of his political activities. So it was only natural that the Democratic county chairman should ask her to replace her husband on the ballot. A tragic air crash took Mort Lloyd's life just twenty days following his primary victory in the 3rd Congressional District. Mrs. Lloyd's subtle business acumen, sensitivity, and love of people made her an attractive candidate. She accepted, and won with 52 percent of the vote. She became the first woman ever to be elected by popular vote to the Congress from Tennessee. Mrs. Lloyd was re-elected to a second term in November 1976 with 58 percent of the vote.

Congresswoman Lloyd has a long list of firsts. She was the first woman to serve on the Select Committee on Aging; the first woman to ever serve on the prestigious Science and Technology Committee; and in the 95th session of Congress, is the ranking majority member on the Subcommittee on Fossil and Nuclear Energy Administration. She is a member of the House Public Works and Transportation Committee and a member of the board of directors of the United Democrats in Congress.

The congresswoman also introduced a measure to equalize the tax treatment of single taxpayers when they are not dependents of their parents. "This measure," she says, "will help to lower the tax burden on single people, many of whom are just entering the job market, or elderly people living on retirement incomes." She adds, "The single person who works, whether unmarried, divorced, or widowed, pays approximately 20 percent more in taxes than the taxpayer who qualifies as head-of-household. This is neither fair nor reasonable, and I hope that among the other needed changes in the tax laws, the Congress will enact this bill."

This two-term congresswoman also reintroduced a bill she sponsored in the last Congress calling for the imposition of mandatory jail sentences for felonies committed with a hand gun. "Under this bill," she explains, "anyone found guilty of a crime involving the use of hand guns would automatically be sentenced to a minimum of five years in jail, without parole or probation, for the first offense and ten years for a subsequent crime. This kind of automatic jail term will put the burden on the criminal who abuses the right to own a hand gun, and not on innocent, law-abiding gun owners," she outlines.

Congresswoman Lloyd is one of the many women who succeeded their late husbands in Congress, and she would like the record to be made clear. "You know that most people believe that when a wife succeeds her husband in Congress, she merely takes off her apron and leaves the kitchen," she says with a slight grimace. "If this were true, we wouldn't last a minute. Most of us worked with our husbands, shared their interests, and were qualified to assume the seat. I walked many miles campaigning, worked in his office, and made speeches when my husband's schedule was too full. So it's really being prepared, qualified, and involved that causes women to replace their husbands," she concludes with a tone of conviction ringing in her voice.

Like most congresswomen, Mrs. Lloyd does not believe a law background is essential. Knowledge of the law is helpful in some areas. "But when it comes to areas like energy committees, I think it's helpful that we have a Ph.D. in the field of nuclear energy or physics on our committees. We have farmers as members on agricultural committees. I think we need to have people who are knowledgeable in fields other than the law. In any case, a degree in law doesn't prepare you for the job." Being aware of the issues that are of state, national, and international significance is vital. A member of Congress must be in attendance to have this knowledge. Just ask Congresswoman Lloyd. She has maintained one of the highest records of voter participation in Congress with a 99.9 percent score in the 94th Congress.

Marilyn Lloyd takes her responsibility quite seriously,

like the other congresswomen. She keeps her constituents up-to-date on the bills she supports or opposes and the reasons for her actions. Her *Reports to the Third District* go to every one of her constituents three times a year. She polls her constituents with an annual questionnaire at the beginning of each year to get their feelings about congressional issues. In addition, the congresswoman maintains a full schedule of services to each of the communities in the 3rd District. She publishes a list of times and places where her representatives can be reached. When not busy in Washington on weekends, she returns to her district office. During the 1974 Congress, Congresswoman Lloyd spent seventy-four of the ninety weekends in the district. So that she can be even more available to the people, she holds periodic "Town Hall Meetings" where she welcomes the chance to hear about her constituents' concerns.

With all of these activities, one wonders how Mrs. Lloyd manages to maintain a sense of family life. She has four children: Nancy, 29, Debbie, 26, Mari, 21, and Morty, 13. "The only way it can work is to make your children a very important part of your life and work. When I was asked to run, I brought my children together, and we held a family conference. They helped me with the decision and participated in the campaign. Morty, who attends junior-high school, does volunteer work too. There are some disadvantages to maintaining what one might call a 'normal' family life, of course. But the advantages outweigh them by far. They've had opportunities to meet many people and participate in activities that aren't usually available to young people. We're a very close family. Sometimes I jokingly say that my children really take care of me. I plan very carefully so there's time to spend with my young son."

When asked about leisure-time activities, the congresswoman replies. "This work is my hobby." She laughs easily.

"It's a seven-day-week job. But I managed to go to basketball games with Morty, and I read continuously." She thinks for a moment. "One of the first things I learned when I came to Washington was that one must establish a strict time schedule. There are so many things to do, places to go, and interests that you want to pursue. But you only have so much energy. So you must establish priorities."

Congresswoman Lloyd sees women gaining in the decision-making process. "There won't be any revolutionary changes overnight. But we are approaching the time when women will be judged by their merits. I wouldn't want to be accepted or given priority because I'm a token woman. I want people to say—'Marilyn Lloyd is a capable woman.' "

Women are needed in the political field. But Mrs. Lloyd sees them as individuals, not as bringing any special, sex-related talents to the running of our government. "I think that there are tremendous numbers of women who are very refreshing and contribute a great deal to public life. But the individual concept holds. Those who are capable, talented, and articulate can get the job done. It is such a tragedy, when we think of the brain power we've lost as a country in the past 200 years by not taking advantage of the abilities of women. I think basically women are extremely level-headed."

How does the congresswoman feel about the possibility of her own children entering public life careers? "I would be very pleased," she replies with enthusiasm. "When I was sworn in the 94th Congress in 1975, my son was on the floor with me. He was a bit younger then, of course. I said to him, 'Son, I hope that you can be here twenty or twenty-five years from now repeating the oath." He looked around and saw some of the younger members of Congress and said, 'Oh Momma. I don't think it will take me that long!' But there again, I made a mistake . . . the old stereotyping thing! I have a very capable, intelligent daughter who's getting a double major in business and economics in college. So perhaps my Mari will be the one to take her mother's place, and I will encourage her in that direction. She'll graduate next April and will probably go on to law school. Her background will be ideal. I'm teaching her now to become very involved in politics. She's active in the Young Democrats on campus at UTC."

Congresswoman Lloyd would like young people to know that there is little glamor attached to life in Washington. It's a hard life and very demanding of you, both emotionally and physically. Sometimes you lie awake at night thinking about votes, bills, and issues. "You must have an incredibly deep love of people. I'm a preacher's daughter, and I was brought up to love people because God created them. In that, every day we are helping people—whether it be a social security problem, someone who needs food stamps, or admission to a Veterans' Administration Hospital, or help understanding legislation. But I think the rewards are equal to the hard work. This can be a very rewarding career, if one wants to give service," the congresswoman concludes convincingly.

Congresswoman Lloyd plans to continue serving the needs of the people of Tennessee. Perhaps one day, Mari will serve with her or succeed her in the House.

Helen Stevenson Meyner

Mrs. Helen Meyner is no stranger to the world of politics and politicians. Her decision to run for the House of Representatives came after twenty years of involvement in New Jersey politics. In 1956, she worked for her cousin, the late Senator and presidential candidate, Adlai Stevenson. Actually, it was during this presidential campaign that she met her future husband. "I worked very hard for Adlai Stevenson—not only because he was a relative, but because I believed in him and thought he was an excellent candidate." Admiration is reflected in her tone of voice. "I was working in New York then and went home to spend the weekend with my family. My father was president of Oberlin College at the time." As a matter of fact, William E. Stevenson was president of Oberlin from 1946 to 1961. The following year, he was appointed ambassador to the Philippines and served for three years, 1962 to 1965.

Congresswoman Meyner shifts to a more comfortable position on the sofa before she continues. "I had never met the governor of New Jersey, but my husband-to-be was giving the keynote speech at a mock convention of Oberlin students. And that's how I really met Governor Robert Meyner." She pauses to smile. "The governor was a guest in my parents' home. I remember we met in May 1955, and were married in January 1957, while he was serving his first term as governor."

He served as governor from 1953 to 1962. Mrs. Meyner is quite at home in this Capitol setting with her political expertise gained first as cousin to an able American statesman and then as wife of the governor of New Jersey.

Despite her experience, Helen Meyner was not successful in her first attempt to win public office. Although she led the Democratic Party ticket in 1972, her 13th District was a traditionally Republican stronghold. However, Mrs. Meyner was not discouraged. She campaigned vigorously again for a seat in the 94th Congress. She won a decisive victory in her second attempt. For women, winning elections often proves less difficult than gaining the nomination. Sometimes women have to resort to methods other than the traditional ones to gain support. An example of this is drawing upon the backing of all women's groups or choosing controversial issues that might carry financial support as a bonus. If a woman chooses to create a separate organization to run her own primary race, she needs money. More money is needed to maintain the organization until the general election. If she wins the election, she certainly can't expect any major support from the traditional party. So gaining support for primaries and elections is a difficult task for women politicians.

Representative Meyner doesn't feel that there is a special kind of preparation for a potential public service career. "Of course," she explains, "I think it helps to study politics, political science. . . . It helps to be a lawyer in many ways, although that isn't necessary. In some aspects, there are too many lawyers here in Congress." She laughs lustily. "What we need are more poets, artists, and pipe-fitters. Congress should represent all aspects of a very diverse society, which this country certainly is."

A review of Congresswoman Meyner's record proves this point. Born in New York on March 5, 1929 to Eleanor Blumstead Stevenson and William Edward Stevenson, Helen was raised in New York City. She attended elementary and secondary schools in New York and Connecticut. In 1950, she earned a bachelor of arts degree from Colorado College where she majored in history. Later, the congresswoman was awarded an honorary doctor of laws degree from Colorado College and additional honorary doctorates from Lafayette College and Kean College. Mrs. Meyner helped her former husband campaign for re-election as governor. As New Jersey's first lady, she was very active in civic affairs and served as a member of the New Jersey Rehabilitation Commission. Later, she was also designated by the Kennedy administration to report on the problems of our foreign service in Eastern European countries.

When the governor left office in 1962, Mrs. Meyner became a columnist for the Newark *Star Ledger*. She wrote the column for seven years. During this period, she also served on the boards of directors of the Newark Museum, the New Jersey Symphony Orchestra, and the New Jersey Chapter of the United Nations Association. Her interest in public issues was further expressed through another medium—television. She hosted interview shows in Newark and New York where she led discussions of national issues with public officials, authors, and other personalities.

Although no longer the first lady, she continued her interest in politics. Congresswoman Meyner worked throughout New Jersey for both causes and candidates during the 1960s.

She became a member of the New Jersey Democratic Policy Council, served on the board of trustees of Rider College, and worked for numerous charitable organizations.

In her freshman term in Congress, she was assigned to the House International Relations Committee. She also serves on its oversight subcommittee, which has oversight responsibility over the CIA, military aid, the Peace Corps, and all covert intelligence activities. She is gratified by her personal accomplishments in the areas covered by this committee. One example is the Indochina controversy, where she firmly opposed continued military aid to the South Vietnam government.

"In some ways, there are more frustrations than personal satisfactions in being a member of Congress. As one knows, the wheels of government move slowly and at a very deliberate pace. The name of the game is compromise!" She shakes her well-groomed head to express a gloomy reality. "But I think we all try to be of as much service as possible. At least, I know that I do." She thinks for a moment. "I represent almost a half million people in northwestern New Jersey, and I serve them in a variety of ways." Records show that in floor debates, she urged that humanitarian aid to countries involved in the civil war of Southeast Asia be directed through international organizations to guard against misuse of funds, and that free military training for autocratic foreign governments be stopped. She also introduced an amendment on humanitarian assistance which was defeated by a 200 to 200 vote.

The well-known Meyner Amendment is one piece of legislation that gave her great satisfaction. "The amendment wanted to use private and voluntary organizations in bringing relief to all of Vietnam after the war. But unfortunately, it was defeated. But I worked hard on it."

Although her major interests fall in the area of international affairs, Congresswoman Meyner is also concerned with helping the unemployed and the elderly, with providing incentives for small businesses and homeowners, and with social security reforms.

Representative Meyner feels the movement of women to positions of power in government is barely inching along. "As you know, there are no women in the United States Senate and, out of 435 members of the House, there are only eighteen congresswomen! We're down one from last Congress, when there were nineteen. And when you realize that women are 53 percent of the national vote, it's disheartening. In this Congress, if you include the Senate, there are 535 people, so the eighteen aren't very proportionate." The congresswoman points out with emphasis, "There ought to be more women. This is still, in many ways, an exclusive men's club." She sighs. "But it's a very time-consuming job. That makes it hard for a young woman with a family to run for Congress. As one woman ambassador once said, "I don't need a husband in this job—I need a wife!" Meaning, of course, just to fill the roles women are still expected to carry out," Mrs. Meyner says cynically. "For example, when Pat Schroeder first arrived in Washington, a member of the press said to her, 'Mrs. Schroeder here you are a member of Congress and you have two small children. How do you justify that?' Congresswoman Schroeder replied in her usual calm manner. 'Well—I've got a brain and a uterus and I've used them both!' "

For relaxation, Mrs. Meyner and her husband include traveling among other hobbies. Membership on the International Relations Committee permits additional opportunities for this avocation. "We're both avid tennis players. I love and collect antiques, but this takes a lot of time to really browse. So I don't do as much of that any more. I'm in my district every weekend, so that hobbies have to be limited. When I'm there, I make the rounds, give talks, and meet with groups of constituents with a variety of problems and requests. We have very long days here in Washington. They're filled with meetings and appointments. The problem is that you're supposed to be in three places at once."

This congresswoman enjoys her job thoroughly. "It's, in many ways, like going to school. You're reading and learning all the time. You have to deal with such a variety of legislation—everything from natural gas to meetings with prime ministers. Just this morning, I met with the minister of a new South American country—Surinam. There are so many opportunities to add dimensions to your personal growth . . . educationally, emotionally, and socially. You just have to be on top of about everything that is happening."

Congresswoman Meyner is rather statuesque, with sharp piercing eyes set in a finely-boned, handsome face. Her voice has the resonance of a trained contralto with words clearly and beautifully articulated. With her sharp sense of humor, she tells an amusing story of dual roles. "Although I always worked, when my husband used to come home after a long day's work, he'd ask, 'what kind of a day have you had, Helen?' I would say, 'The dog piddled on the new carpet, the cellar is flooded, and our freezer is on the blink.' Now when I get back to New Jersey and my husband on a Friday night, I ask, 'Dear—what kind of week have you had?' And he'll say, 'the dog has run off, you need new vacuum bags, or, we ought to put the screens in.' So in many ways our roles have reversed, although he is a very successful lawyer," Congresswoman Meyner concludes with a jovial laugh.

Barbara A. Mikulski

The social revolution of the 1950s and '60s brought injustices experienced by minorities to the public's attention. These minorities were black, Hispanic, American Indian, and Chicano. But there are other minority groups who are part of the mythical "melting pot." Most are familiar to us because of their food, festivals, and parades. They are first and second generation Poles, Greeks, Slavs, Italians, Irish and Germans. They work hard. They need a voice, and Barbara Mikulski plans to be that voice. She will add that voice to her other voices for the elderly, handicapped, and women—all the minorities of this country.

Home and family are said to be man's most precious belongings. To protect them, a calm, rational person often performs unusual feats of bravery or sudden destruction. Barbara Mikulski chose bravery. There were plans to run a freeway right through her community. That meant tearing down the homes of more than 400 retired and elderly people. Incensed, Miss Mikulski and her neighbors got together to save their homes and businesses. She became one of the organizers of the protest. The group not only held off the highway, but they persuaded the city to build a community park in the path of the freeway. In the process, they launched a community restoration movement in their white, multi-ethnic neighborhoods. Barbara Mikulski became a local celebrity who would fight for her neighbors even beyond the streets of Baltimore.

Miss Mikulski was born in Baltimore, Maryland, on July 20, 1936. She is the eldest of three daughters of William and Christine (Kutz) Mikulski. After graduation from the Institute of Notre Dame High School, she entered Mount Saint Agnes College where she earned a B.A. in 1958. In 1965, she was awarded a Master's Degree from the University of Maryland's School of Social Work. Her area of specialization was community organization. Her interest in people helped to shape her career.

Although she trained for a career in social work, Miss Mikulski was drawn into politics by a local issue—the fight against the freeway. "The community action revealed other problems," Miss Mikulski explains. "We saw other problems related to inadequate schools, libraries, and health services. I decided that rather than knock on the doors of city hall, I'd be more effective inside helping people get their fair share of governmental services." She pauses, "I guess the battle of the expressway and the politicizing of myself really lead to my candidacy.

"At first my family and friends were cautious. They wondered if it would be wise to seek public office. I'm from a community where women aren't expected to enter political careers. It's an older, working-class community. But once they realized my sincerity, my entire family was extremely supportive. My Mom and Dad campaigned actively for me. The whole family mobilized their efforts around me. For example, my two sisters put their babies in carriages and went around knocking on doors. Aunts and uncles and cousins, too, joined in. They converted their neighborhood businesses into mini campaign headquarters. And all of them worked at the polls on Election Day advocating my cause." Miss Mikulski was successful in her campaign, and won a seat on the Baltimore City Council. She served from 1971 to 1976.

Representative Mikulski is a freshman member of Congress. The many tasks, assignments, and complexities of this career are exhausting alone. There are so many things to learn and situations to which one must adjust. Congresswoman Mikulski believes that two types of experiences helped her adjust to her new role. "One was the experiences and values of my family life, reinforced by sixteen years of Catholic education. I was raised in an atmosphere where you really had to help your neighbor. Everyone had a sense of service. You were part of the community. You weren't alone on this planet. There was no 'just do your own thing' attitude! The neighborhood was your home, and the people in it were your family. And I've expanded that thinking into my council district and now into my congressional district." Miss Mikulski rises from behind the desk. She is less than five feet tall, but her spirited manner makes her seem much taller.

"My training as a social worker was an invaluable experience. I knew how to organize and how to analyze public policy, and when I had to advocate causes of my constituency with other legislative committees and the executive branch, I knew foreign languages." She applies a light comic touch. "Like 'bureaucratese', grant funding, and other things—I mean. So I think the combination of growing up in a neighborhood with a strong social conscience and then gaining the training which enabled me to convert those feelings of the people into concrete actions and recommendations were extremely helpful."

A role model can have a strong positive or negative influence upon a young person's development and life. Congresswoman Mikulski speaks fondly of her adolescent years. "In the Catholic schools, I had women as role models. In addition, my mother and aunts were also strong role models. My mother worked in the family grocery store. They demonstrated how one could raise a family, and, at the same time, make a major contribution outside of the home. But the nuns were positive role models too. Many of them had earned Ph.Ds. Some were chemistry professors. Normally girls don't get exposed to such positive images. So I was fortunate enough to see how women could be strong. In my high school and college, I saw women who were talented administrators and intellectuals."

In addition to her public service life, Miss Mikulski was an adjunct professor in the department of sociology at Loyola College from 1972 to 1976. She is a member of the National Women's Political Caucus, Members of Congress for Peace Through Law, the Environmental Study Conference, and the Democratic Study Group. She has lectured at various universities and colleges, including Harvard University, the University of Notre Dame, and Johns Hopkins University.

Representative Mikulski introduced impressive legislature while serving in the city council. "I'm proud of the legislation that created a commission on aging. When I came into the city hall, the older people were under-served. Services to agencies were fragmented through the bureaucracy. There was no real advocate for the aged. By working with the mayor, I was able to create a Commission on Aging and Retirement Education. The acronym spells CARE and that's exactly what it has been doing. Reduced bus fare for the aged was another success. One of the great joys of my life was to go to city hall each morning with the knowledge that old people who had clinic appointments and had to get around town would be able to . . . because of legislation introduced by me. Other legislation included a commission to study the impact on rape victims. At that time, Baltimore women who did report rape were treated like criminals, examined in police stations, and received no medical treatment or supportive services. As a direct result of our commission's study, we were able to bring about changes. Women are now examined in hospitals. The result of the commission's study was then used by me and other women's advocates to bring about changes in state laws related to the use of evidence and criminal procedures in rape cases."

"On the federal level, one of my achievements was to help form the Congressional Women's Caucus, and to begin the development of certain concerted actions which would be helpful to women. I have co-sponsored a variety of bills which range from social security reform to dealing with the use of children in pornography. But probably my most important piece of legislation deals with family violence. This legislation will coordinate the activities of the United States government in a more definitive effort to deal with family violence. The focus will be on battered spouses particularly. I hope that my legislation will create federal initiatives that will help both women and men who are being battered receive much needed assistance. The agency, ACTION, will provide the resources to help women in local communities organize comprehensive services. These include the establishment of shelters and other kinds of supportive services. If this piece of legislation passes by the end of my first term in Congress and millions of battered women are being helped, I'll be very proud."

Congresswoman Mikulski is the first woman to serve on the House Interstate and Foreign Commerce Committee. Her subcommittees include Transportation and Commerce, and Communications. She has also been assigned to the Merchant Marine and Fisheries Committee, with three subcommittees appointments: Merchant Marine, Coast Guard and Navigation, and Oceanography.

Although much of her energies have been directed toward helping women, older people, and other oppressed groups, Miss Mikulski has been very active in her committee assignments that have national influence. "I'm the only woman to serve on the Ad-Hoc Energy Committee which is formulating the national energy policy that will, in many ways, determine the shape and destiny of this country. I've used my background of local community work to play the role of consciousness raiser. My concerns reflect those of the people at the grassroots level. 'How will our policy affect the cost of running a local government?' As the cost of energy rises, there will be a direct effect on our educational and social programs. 'What will it mean to people on fixed incomes?' 'How will an increased gasoline tax affect a program like Meals on Wheels?' This may indirectly force abandonment of a social program. You see, men think in terms of global issues. They are technical-minded, and my questions startled them. So the committee listens and takes these things into consideration." She rests a moment before continuing.

"On the Communications Subcommittee, I'll help rewrite the Communications Act which was written forty-five years ago. When we discuss communications issues, the subjects range from violence on television to navigational aids. My concern about the protection of the environment has been voiced through my other comimttee assignments. I've raised questions on how to maximize safety so that we don't have tankers producing enormous oil spills off our Atlantic and Pacific coasts. These issues are of great concern to me and the general public."

Miss Mikulski is single, attractive, and congenial. Her overt honesty and willingness to confront issues is rarely seen in a freshman member of Congress. But she came to Congress to do a job, and she plans to to do it. Even though it may be costly, in many respects she is willing to sacrifice. "For a woman, a career in public life is indeed costly, and the area affected most is one's social life. In effect, politics becomes your primary relationship. I spend more time with my constituent family than I spend with my real family. That's one of the sad components—the incredible time demands. But I try very hard to tighten my schedule so I can enjoy the theater or time off on a weekend. Unfortunately, this only happens about one out of every six weekends."

Like most other congresswomen, Barbara Mikulski advises young people to get involved in community issues within their communities as an orientation to public life. "Take an issue of interest and start working to try and make government more responsive to the needs of grassroots citizens. They'll get involved quickly in the decision-making process if they do this. That's how I got started. One must feel strongly about the issue selected. Perhaps something they'd like to see changed. For example, young people may feel that there are not enough recreational centers in their neighborhoods. Perhaps the centers close too early or the range of activities is limited. They can round up a group of kids and visit the local elected official. In order to get involved, they must ask 'Who has the power to make the decision in this particular issue?' Young people should form coalition with other groups too. But only by getting out into the community can they be aware of needs, issues and possible support. They will discover that in this country there are two kinds of power. There's power that comes from high status and wealth. And there's power that is derived from a group of people dedicated to a single purpose trying to bring about change. Young people can attend meetings of the PTA, community, school, and library boards, and let members know of their needs which will enable them to become full participating citizens."

Congresswoman Mikulski is one of those who was inspired by the late President John F. Kennedy. She observed the positive definition of politics in action. At the moment, her plan is to remain in Congress where she hopes to do the best job possible. She's happy and enjoys her new life as a congresswoman.

The best thing about being a congresswoman is the position of power. "I like power which brings about change. Many people are afraid of power, but the only time you have to be afraid is when there are no checks and balances in your own life. This prevents you from limiting your associations to other power-holders only. You must get out and listen to the people and get other viewpoints. This means holding press conferences, town meetings, and meetings with high school students. Making yourself available to people in general is the rule. But to know that you sit on a committee which will help improve the resources that will go to city governments or bring new public access to the media is very rewarding."

All facets are not happy ones in the life of a member of Congress. The intricate, slow process of getting legislation passed is disappointing to Miss Mikulski. "I'd like to have a meeting on the subject, discuss possible action, and pass the law two days later. Just the process, for example, of drafting my battered women legislation took almost two months of continuous work on the part of one of my aides. Then we'll introduce it, and it will go to hearings. It will be six months to one year before my legislation is enacted." Of course, the lack of personal time is also a disappointment. There are so many demands made upon you. "Perhaps my greatest disappointment is the fact that I can't find a Xerox machine that could reproduce me and have me in all the places I'd like to be."

For young women who seek careers in public life, Barbara

Mikulski advises, "They have to decide upon an area in which they can be the most helpful. Some people have advocate personalities, and perhaps their best role would be grassroots organizers or members of legislature. Get started with real people's problems at this level as a beginning. One of the reasons I'm so effective here in influencing my colleagues on the issues of family violence is they know that I was a social worker. They listen to me, because they appreciate my knowledge of child welfare and child neglect. I spent years working with juvenile courts. I went into prisons and helped to reunite families and witnessed these emotional contacts. Other women prefer a more service oriented role. So they should select those areas in which they can be of service. And we need good teachers, guidance counselors and social workers desperately. Then again there are areas which are not in direct contact with people and may seem non-traditional, but they help people too. Public administrators, accountants, managers, and fiscal advisers are excellent examples. Perhaps some young women will find these areas challenging. They can work for the government on local, state, or federal levels."

She peers out of the window before continuing. "It was so helpful for me, when I was a member of the Baltimore City Council, to have as the chief fiscal adviser another woman. She knew those budgets inside and out, and knew how to help me to move the funds around to help people. So we need women in public service from a variety of orientations. A girl shouldn't think that if she's a CPA, it means working in corporate firms, banks, or the media. Even there, they have public affairs programs so there's incredible opportunity now for women." There is a reflective pause. "But as they move in, I would hope that they also think about all the other women who need help."

Looking back to 1957, there was no women's movement.

There were no affirmative action programs. So there has been progress. As Congresswoman Mikulski looks ahead to 1997, she offers these words. "For all of us who have struggled to begin this 'rope ladder' climb, I hope the next generation of women have an easier time. But they should remember their obligation to women in their generation and the women to follow. One of the most disappointing things I heard were the remarks made by the first female Rhodes scholarship winner. She is reported to have said, 'I'm not one of those pro-woman types.' Well, she would never have been chosen, if it hadn't been for all of those brave women who had gone before her advocating the cause. And their names are Abzug, Holtzman, and so many others."

It takes conscious decisions to involve yourself in a community or political organization process. Often the decision is a soul-searching one. Congresswoman Mikulski relates an incident which took place in 1963, when she was a welfare worker. The civil rights movement was in full swing, and a march on Washington was planned. "All my friends and colleagues in the Department of Welfare were going to participate. I chose not to go, because I was afraid. I was afraid of violence, getting hurt. Also I was afraid of ridicule from other friends. I just couldn't involve myself in such a dramatic, public action. You see, it was one thing to be for civil rights on a coffee-break, but quite another thing to go marching on the Capitol. So I didn't go. And that day, as I went around making my home visits, people were watching their televisions. They were watching the March on Washington! And I was overcome by the outpouring of people's feelings and organizational effort. I sat in people's homes and observed their intense involvement. And I did something that was quite unusual for me. I walked off the job and went home, because I was overcome by what I was seeing. And I watched Martin Luther

King give his 'I Have A Dream' speech and I felt ashamed of myself. I vowed then and there that if I ever felt strongly about an issue, I would never be a non-participating observer. I would never sit on the sidelines again . . . I'd go where the action was!" Congresswoman Mikulski has kept that vow.

Patsy T. Mink

Patsy Takemoto Mink has had her share of *firsts*. But strong will, determination, and intelligence have helped her overcome some of the roadblocks which face forerunners who break down traditional barriers. She has learned to use defeat as a way of re-arming for the next struggle. This attractive Japanese-American woman was born in Paia, a village on Mauri Island. Her father, Suematsu Takemoto, graduated from the University of Hawaii with a degree in civil engineering.

Like some of her colleagues, Mrs. Mink's interest in politics really began in high school. She was elected president of the student body and was later named valedictorian of her 1944 graduating class. One of her heroes was the family physician, so she followed a pre-med major at the University of Hawaii. After earning her degree in zoology and chemistry, Patsy Mink had second thoughts about a medical career. Occasionally, even back in 1948, a minority status can be an advantage. The University of Chicago Law School accepted her application as a foreign student; someone in the admissions office did not know that people born in Hawaii are American citizens, and have been since 1898.

When Mrs. Mink returned home in 1952, no established law firm considered the fledgling, female lawyer even worthy of a law clerkship. But this didn't deter Patsy—she opened a one-person law firm. To kill time between clients, who were mostly non-paying, she became active in the Democratic party. Patsy was deeply concerned about Hawaii's quest for statehood. Many local residents were urging this move and congressional members appeared supportive. Hawaii was basically a one-party state—Republican. Patsy Mink, a Democrat, joined with other young professionals returning home to create change in governing Hawaii. The tropical paradise is composed of seven populated islands. The young Democrats needed organizational structure with a program for their energies. Patsy Mink provided some of that direction by organizing the group, and by 1954, the Democrats became strong enough to gain control of the legislature . . . the first time since 1898.

During the 1954 campaign, Mrs. Mink got her initiation into politics by performing all the routine tasks of telephoning, ringing door bells, handing out leaflets, and mapping out strategic spots for speaking schedules. Two years later, she decided to run for the territorial House of Representatives. Since she wasn't known outside of the political structure, and since she was not a native of Honolulu, she had no following. Her family supported her efforts and contributed as much as possible. "I don't know if any particular person gave me the most encouragement. But if I had to single out one person, I guess it would be my husband, John Mink. He had been an active Democrat in Jim Thorpe, Pennsylvania," she recalls.

Although she had no great financial backing nor local labor support, Mrs. Mink proved that she could be a winner. She worked very hard chairing committees in the Young

Democrats Club to demonstrate her capability. Very few women were involved in party politics, so she was rather a novelty. "My family was lukewarm about my campaigning— perhaps because they thought I might lose and bring shame upon the family name. They hesitated to get too committed. But I had about ten to twelve friends, and we eventually created local interest in my political activities."

As for preparation for membership in Congress, Mrs. Mink says, "My law degree gave the voters confidence that I could do the job. And my organizational activities and involvement in the national Young Democrats as a whole provided the necessary experience in national issues." She pauses. "But I had been in elective office in the state legislature from 1956 to 1958, and then a member of the state senate from 1962 to 1964. All of this gave me sufficient legislative background to qualify for a seat in Congress."

When Patsy Mink came to Washington, she became the eighth sitting congresswoman in the 89th Congress. "It wasn't that the men weren't receptive, but we were so few and so unique. Our viewpoints, interests, and commitments were quite different from theirs. And, of course, there was no collective spirit among us, which didn't help. My ethnic background added to my uniqueness. I can't say that this made life more difficult, but I certainly stood out in committee and group meetings with my colleagues." There is slight ironic humor in the tone of her voice.

Congresswoman Mink, at age thirty-six, became the first woman from the fiftieth state to be elected to the Congress. It is said that she celebrated the event by painting in the missing eye on her *darum* doll, an old Japanese custom. The doll, considered a good luck symbol, is bought without eyes. At the beginning of a new undertaking, one eye is painted in. When success is achieved, the owner paints in the other eye. This doll is also unique in that it cannot be knocked down.

Initially elected at-large, she was elected to represent the 2nd Congressional District, which comprises all the neighboring islands and all zip codes in Hawaii other than the city of Honolulu. This district includes the windward and leeward sides of Oahu, Hawaii, Maui, Lolokai, Kauai, Lanai, and Nihau. Of her constitutents, 40 percent were Caucasians, 30 percent were Japanese, and 30 percent were comprised of other ethnic groups.

Congresswoman Mink was an early champion for women's rights. In 1963, she pioneered for one of the earliest "equal pay for equal work" laws in the United States. "I learned very early in Congress that I held triple responsibilities—to my constituents back home who elected me and to all of the women of America. Also, I felt a great sense of responsibility to the ethnic minority whom I represented. I knew that the future of many hinged upon what I did, what I said, and how successful I was. This made the job more challenging and, of course, taxing." With this sense of obligation, Congresswoman Mink could not afford errors. "I decided early that whatever course of action I followed (it) would be a very important one. Whether I won or lost would not be consequential, but the statement on the issue itself would be significant. Also, I selected those issues which I was certain would yield results. This would allow people to easily weigh the effectiveness of my representation," she adds.

Women have been taken seriously from the moment they arrived in Congress, Mrs. Mink believes. And her reasons are somewhat different from those of other congresswomen. "You see," she begins, "they are listened to much more than any single male representative. Male members are heeded if they have power and authority through membership on important committees or hold chairmanships of these committees. But women, regardless of whether they occupy such positions of importance, are listened to, by and large. Women represent and speak out for a larger constituency than the regular congressperson, and the male members realize this. I believe women are held in very high esteem by their male colleagues. There is an implicit recognition that the women who made it had to be ten times as good as the men, because it is acknowledged that it is extremely difficult for women to be elected to high office."

Congresswomen can be effective in any area, Mrs. Mink believes. "I think that when women speak out on matters of humanitarian concern or on basic issues such as equality, civil rights, or justice, they are more likely to be afforded attention. They may champion other causes which are equally important, but, for some reason, women are identified with the latter." The Representative from Hawaii's record attests to this practice. In Congress, Mrs. Mink authored and sponsored the Women's Educational Equity Act Bill that was signed into law in 1974. The first of its kind, the legislation provided up to $30,000,000 a year for a three-year period for projects and activities geared toward increasing educational and job opportunities for women. She also authored an omnibus civil rights bill for women (H.R. 7444) that adds prohibitions against discrimination on the basis of sex to those laws already on the books that only prohibit discrimination on the basis of color, race, religion, or national origin. The bill, unfortunately, died in committee. Congresswoman Mink fought equally hard in areas of equal credit opportunity, child care legislation, tax laws that discriminate against women, Title IX of the Education Amendments of 1972 (barring sex discrimination in federal programs and activities in most educational institutions), and civil rights enforcement.

Appointed to the powerful House Education and Labor Committee in her first term, she has been able to influence and author important legislation in the field of education, particularly on the elementary and secondary levels. Federal dollars for education have always been one of her highest priorities, and her efforts have kept millions of dollars flowing into Hawaii annually. Her special interests have centered on bilingual education, education for the handicapped, school lunch programs, emergency school aid to meet the special needs of schools trying to eliminate segregation, and impact aid—additional federal aid to schools with large numbers of federal civilian and military employees.

Congresswoman Mink sees no conflict in reconciling the roles of wife, mother, career woman, and politician. "Obviously, you have to be willing to work three times as hard because there are three jobs to be done—each quite different from the other." John Francis Mink, her husband, is an engineer who specializes in hydrology and geology. His talent is much in demand and provides a great deal of flexibility and mobility. He accepted a fellowship at Johns Hopkins University when the family first moved to Washington. He has been a consultant in water development, mainly in the Pacific area. Mr. Mink acts as campaign manager and political advisor, but the congresswoman makes the final decisions herself.

Congresswoman Mink found her years in Congress most productive and satisfying. "There have been all kinds of rewards in terms of jobs, tasks, and projects which have been achieved as a result of personal involvement. Incidents like cases won in court, bills enacted which I have written, changes made in programs because of my personal direction, and individuals whose hardships were softened because of intervention on my part have all made the job worthwhile. My entire career has been an exceedingly exciting and challenging experience."

As for her greatest achievement in Congress, Mrs. Mink selected one case. "It was a case in which twenty-three other members of Congress joined with me in suing five federal agencies for refusing to release information regarding the nuclear underground tests in the Aleutians. Our case went all the way to the Supreme Court. As a result of our case, we were able to establish guidelines for later amendments to the Freedom of Information Act. It is now possible for individual citizens to obtain information from their government. The litigation was cited numerous times by the government lawyers when they presented their brief and argument before the Supreme Court in their efforts to obtain the Watergate tapes from the president of the United States—Richard M. Nixon. The Supreme Court delivered a unanimous opinion that the tapes be released. The release of the tapes ultimately led, for the first time, to the resignation of a president of the United States while in office."

The Representative from Hawaii is quite content with her performance in the House. "I can't think of any facet of my life which I would have done differently. Actually all the pieces have fallen in together quite well. One event in my life laid the foundation for the next experience to be that much more productive.

"To be a really successful female politician, a girl should seek out some specialty and become an expert in that area. A generalist can't make it." Congresswoman Mink advises a good education, broad interests, and community activities as a beginning. The best preparation is participation on the grassroots level. A prospective politician should get to know her constituency and their problems, and try to solve them at this level. She should take an active interest in the day-to-day activities in all the various units of government in the local community. This kind of background is invaluable for a successful career in later years." She pauses momentarily. "Of course, she needs emotional support. Mine comes from my husband, family, and daughter. My father passed away several years ago, so it's my mother who encourages me now."

Women participate fully in the democratic process now in

that they register, vote, and involve themselves in local community activities. They have an input into all the elements of change which take place in our society. "Where women have stopped short is running for political office because of the hazards and the controversies which are all a part of elective politics. Women simply have to decide that they want this kind of life. And until more do, they're not going to be called upon to have a heavy involvement in policy-making."

The progress in our society bears no relationship to getting men to understand the needs of women, according to Mrs. Mink. "Women need to understand themselves, relate to other women, become fully aware of their abilities and potentials, and help other women fight for career opportunities. They need to support other women in campaigns, seek office themselves, too, and try to find fulfillment of their ambitions. I think women can do more for other women, and when they do, women will come to the age of equal participation and fulfillment of their abilities."

Congresswoman Mink gave up her safe House seat to run unsuccessfully for the 1976 Democratic nomination for the United States Senate from Hawaii. This was not her first taste of defeat, but, like the earlier incident, she is not discouraged. "I certainly have no intentions of discarding my interest in politics or discontinuing my political life. One doesn't do that simply by not being an elected politician. Politics to me is a constant involvement in the day-to-day working of your society as a whole, one part of which is government. And I certainly intend to be active in that vein. If the time comes for another opportunity and it seems appropriate, I will certainly run again."

Closing the interview, the congresswoman singles out the important role John Mink has played in her life. "In measuring the experiences and difficulties that I have had in twenty years of elective politics, I would have to note that my husband in many ways has had to endure about as many inconveniences and difficulties in the course of my career as I have. I think young women must be made aware of the great importance of their husbands' participation in their career plans, because a husband's involvement is inevitable when a wife has a political life." Mrs. Mink recalls an incident that took place when she was a freshman in Congress. "The newly elected members of Congress were invited to the White House for dinner with President Johnson. And we all went in and sat down to enjoy a marvelous dinner. After the dinner, the president requested all the congressmen to meet in the East Room for a brief discussion of some important issues. So all the men got up and I was the only female member of the freshman class, so I joined them. This was a dinner party to which our spouses had been invited. Just as I was the only woman to be in the East Room with the congressmen, similarly my husband was left behind with all the wives. The group of about eighty-five women and John Mink went upstairs to the living quarters of the White House to have tea and cookies with the first lady. As the group mingled about and toured the rooms, one of the wives approached my husband and whispered, 'Are you a member of the Secret Service?' "

Just as Mrs. Mink predicted, she is to remain an active politician involved in public life. On March 23, 1977, *The New York Times* reported "The Senate today confirmed President Carter's nomination of former Representative Patsy T. Mink, Democrat of Hawaii, to be an assistant secretary of state. Mrs. Mink will have responsibility for oceans and for international environmental and scientific affairs."

Mary Rose Oakar

Sometimes it's the worship of a hero or heroine, a much admired teacher, or the example set by a family member that influences a young person's career direction. In Congresswoman Oakar's case, it was concern about the environment . . . her own neighborhood. The neighborhood, an old one in the heart of Cleveland, Ohio, was undergoing a too familiar pattern of gradual decline. "When you've always lived in an area, gone to its schools, and hold many fond memories of your childhood in that environment, you are very sensitive to the changes. So it was natural for me to join with friends and neighbors to fight inner-city decay. Something had to be done by us, because we felt our ward representative didn't care very much about our plight." The freshman congresswoman sips a cold soft drink. The temperature has changed suddenly, as it frequently does in Washington. No one is prepared for the warm, humid weather. The congresswoman makes herself comfortable in a large, over-stuffed chair and continues.

"I grew up in a fascinating neighborhood which could be

called a 'miniature America.' There were whites, blacks, Latins, Jews, Moslems, and Christians . . . Catholics and non-believers too. Middle and low-income families lived peacefully together. There were even a few families of wealth around also. Yet as blocks deteriorated to the level of federally defined poverty areas, concern grew among many families. Some, like my own, had been in the community for a couple of generations. My friends, some of them former schoolmates, decided I should take the leadership. I was teaching then." Representative Oakar inhales deeply and then laughs suddenly. "So I ran for city council and won." Her light-hearted manner doesn't disguise a deep involvement and care for people's problems.

The congresswoman's ability to lead was discovered by her classmates in high school. They elected her class president. At Ursuline College, a small woman's school in Cleveland, she was class president for three years and later president of the student body. "I used to think that perhaps they couldn't get anyone else to do the work." Mary Rose Oakar is also modest.

"Probably my mother, who died recently, had the greatest influence upon my life. She was a really terrific person. She was supportive in every one of my ventures." Her voice grows soft. "My mother was a librarian, and when she married my dad in 1931, she gave up what might have been a very rewarding career. She had experience as a buyer for a department store—Higbee Company. And she loved her work. But she gave it all up to devote herself to her home and family. My father was a hard-working, family man. They had five children in nine years . . . all born at home. They probably couldn't afford anything else, but they cherished each other."

Miss Oakar reveals these intimacies in an honest, open manner. It is clear that she is proud of her heritage. She sips her drink. "After my father died, my mother increased her hours of community work. She had more time to give to the neighborhood. The residents appreciated her conscientiousness and asked her to become precinct committeewoman. This was amazing, since she wasn't political and had no background for that kind of activity. So you see, before I got into politics, she was already doing the work of a committeewoman. By calling city hall, she got garbage collected and street lights repaired. Her results were remarkable! She exerted a tremendously stabilizing influence on the neighborhood." The congresswoman is about to discuss her own entry into politics, but she remembers an interesting incident.

"There was a split in the local party groups. My work on neighborhood advisory boards for community action programs was well known. I gave input into how federal funds could be used. I was admired as a teacher too. The dissidents planned to nominate me with full knowledge that my mother would not vote against her daughter. So, in a way, my mother's reluctance to engage in any deceptive practices led to my election as ward leader. All of a sudden, I was thrust into this role that I had never envisioned. So I became the ward leader! But the next year, I ran for councilwoman and won." Her laughter is robust and characteristic of her natural good humor. She adds that this campaign introduced her to some of the vile tactics used by opponents to influence voters. She was the victim of racial and sexual lies which could have ruined a weaker and less known candidate. A pained expression crosses her face, as she recalls the disgraceful incidents. This experience made her aware of the need for ethical conduct in all office seekers and holders.

Congresswoman Oakar represented Ward Eight on the Cleveland city council from 1973 to 1976. During those years, her accomplishments were varied and numerous:

established annual "Community Home Days"

provided for Dial-A-Bus for senior citizens

urged more police protection where there was a high
density of senior citizens

authorized a study to evaluate the sentencing practices
of judges

reorganization of the fire department (planning and
equipment)

introduced a ten-point truancy plan

implemented low interest 3 percent loan program for the
rehabilitation of housing

introduced the resolution to save the Carnegie West
Library

urged a study of "red lining" practices in Cleveland
banks

urged the department of H.E.W. to refund bilingual
programs

requested the prosecution of parents of juveniles who
vandalize public property

requested new recreation centers

Her untiring service did not go unnoticed. She received community recognition awards from the Office of Economic Opportunity, Club San Lorenzo, and the American Indian Center and was given the Nationalities Service Award. Her interest in children led to the founding of a recreational and
cultural arts program for youngsters, five to eighteen years
of age. She also served on boards of trustees for the Federation for Community Planning, Health and Planning Commission, Community Information Service, Society for Crippled
Children, Nationalities Service Center, and Y.W.C.A.

Congresswoman Oakar comes to the House thirty-seven
years after Frances Payne Bolton—the first woman to serve
from Ohio. Although their political affiliations and social

positions differ, Miss Oakar is an admirer of the famous fighter for the people's rights. She was outspoken and often controversial, but never compromised her position to fight for the improved status of women, minors, and minorities. Miss Oakar is a fighter too. She holds strong and definite beliefs and cannot be swayed for expediency or personal gain.

In the primary election, eleven men opposed her. She fought them with hard work and dedication, despite her limited campaign funds. "You know, women in general are not tied into special interest groups. Conducting a campaign is a luxury trip. So for these reasons, women have a hard time raising money. Just to mail postal cards to Democrats in my district cost $10,000. There is discrimination in giving, too. Here's an example. I received a union endorsement, both at the local and state levels, which pleased me very much. Another candidate was given political support too, but the candidate was male. When the checks were issued, mine was for $500 and his amounted to $2,000. So men are still recognized as *the* candidate over women where it counts—in the wallets! Although I'm still in debt personally because of the campaign, over 85 percent of my contributions were under fifty dollars. This pleases me."

Among the solutions offered by Miss Oakar is one that suggests women join with men in a more organized way. This will help to equalize contributions. She also feels that most women are unaware of the costs of campaigning, even at the local level. "Women must focus on the issues that they agree upon. Very often, women dilute their strengths by diversity. For instance, if you are against abortion, that's your position. But you must respect a differing opinion. Don't fight it! Go on to something bigger where you can join hands. I believe strongly in the Equal Rights Amendment. Some women are frightened by it. But that's not the only issue. We should be concerned about job discrimination, equal access to education and employment, and recognition of woman as builders of society. Our concerns should involve the homemaker, the senior citizen, and the professional. They're all involved, although on different levels. E.R.A. means equal opportunity to grow, develop, and reach one's full capabilities."

Women need to be educated about other aspects too. "I feel we should mobilize women around issues which foster better government. Ethics, moral conduct, and personal sacrifice are just a few of the principles that are important. Everyone can identify with these."

The freshman congresswoman has already had her baptism of fire on the floor. She won her first fight because she took a stand and maintained it. She relates the incident like this. "Congress had a chance to establish a National Commission on Neighborhoods—designed to preserve, protect, and defend the quality of neighborhoods like my own back in Cleveland. The House and Senate appoint two members each and the president selects sixteen. The bill asks that the president's appointees be selected for racial, ethnic, and geographic representation. But, as usual, there is no mention of male-female equality in these appointments. In 1976, we had more than a thousand advisory committees with some 12,000 members . . . 88 percent of those members were men. In a world where 53 percent of the voters are women, it doesn't make much sense. When I brought up the subject in committee, it was rejected. I didn't object then but waited to bring it up again as an amendment on the House floor. Members would have to take a stand then. They would have to think about the women they represent as their votes are recorded in the *Congressional Record*. Of course, I had to fight behind the scenes to get the needed support. I appealed to other members on the simple basis of fairness and consistency with federal regulations. I lobbied everywhere, and I won."

Her greatest disappointment so far has been the attitudes

of some congressmen toward women. "The higher up you go in office, the more narrow the attitudes become," she says sadly. "One has to become a hard-core feminist . . . when personally, all I want to do is a good job. Just imagine that in 1977—I had to offer an amendment to have equal numbers of men and women on advisory committees to neighborhoods. It's incredible! I expected it to be much more open."

The congresswoman thinks that women's groups could and should monitor seats at all levels of government. "In 1976, there were fifty-five open seats in the House where an incumbent was not running. And only five women entered these races. I was one of them. Most of the women who ran faced incumbents and had a real handicap, in addition to the usual ones. But just think of all of those opportunities women had open to them!" She pauses and a somber expression appears on her attractive face. "This is an area where women's organizations can help other women who are considering public office. They can provide information, guidance, and coordinate fund-raising. Their watching House and Senate vacancies and then searching out qualified candidates whom they can support will make a difference. And all things being equal, women can win. I believe traditionally most women work harder than some male opponents to wipe out so called disadvantages of being a woman."

Miss Oakar has no ambitions for higher office at the moment. "What I would like to do with my life is go wherever there is a need. I felt strongly about the need to be a fine educator, and I think I succeeded as a teacher. I enjoyed the arts and made a contribution there. I used my talents in public service too."

She would appreciate time for some kind of a social life. This twenty-four hour job prohibits most traditional dating. She loves the opera and dramatic arts, but duty has to come first, at least for now. She laughs at the contradictory press release which pictures her as highly desirable but unavailable.

The congresswoman advises young people to get involved in politics while in high school. Join campaigns, even local ones, she urges. Begin by just ringinig bells and passing out handbills. She warns youth not to become apathetic. After all, politics really means being concerned with government. A sense of self-confidence is vital. "I remember when my mother had been precinct committeewoman for eight terms, this young man of about twenty-one filed to run against her. I was furious at this young upstart, but my mother didn't seem upset at all. In fact, she took him around and introduced him to the neighbors. She was happy to see a young person involved in community affairs. He got about eight votes, but, more important, he gained by her display of unselfishness. Again I think this is one of the positives women bring to public life. They're not status driven or power thirsty. They enter politics to serve."

Self-confidence and self-discipline were an integral part of Mary Rose Oakar's training. A warm, happy family created a secure sense of self which will help her in the days to come.

Shirley N. Pettis

Mrs. Pettis is the prototype of all the beauty queens who represent California every year in Atlantic City in the Miss America pageant. Unlike most beauty queens, she is intelligent, well-informed, and a shrewd businesswoman. Before entering Congress, the talented representative managed two multi-million dollar businesses: Magnetic Tape Duplicators, at that time the world's largest user and duplicator of magnetic tape, and Audio-Digest. The latter is a non-profit organization which furnishes monthly educational tapes to physicians to keep them abreast of new developments in their fields. This successful enterprise was given outright to the California Medical Association and the millions of dollars in profits go to support needy medical students.

Although Mrs. Pettis personally entered elective politics in 1975, her preparation goes back a long way. She received her first lessons as a child. "I was the only child of a professor of political science and American history. My father had an earned doctorate and was chairman of the department of history," she says in a whispery, lyrical voice. "From the time I learned to talk, many of our conversations were geared to what was going on in the country and the world. Although I didn't realize it, at that early age, I'm sure these talks were very influential in shaping my interest in the field." She continues after a short pause. This is a very busy day in the House. Votes will be taken on at least one critical issue. Congresswoman Pettis has left the floor for this brief interview. She is breathless but gracious.

"Before I came to Congress, I was in business with my husband, and we learned to work as a team. I managed the electronics company which we started. This permitted my husband to follow his other interests. But this innate curiosity and concern about world affairs has been with me throughout life." The combination of astute judgment and profound political skill made her an outstanding potential candidate upon the sudden, tragic death of her husband.

Mrs. Pettis was able to draw upon other talents, too. In college, she had been a journalism major. In her husband's first term in Congress, she wrote a weekly news column called, *From Your Congressman's Wife.* It was carried in California papers. It was non-partisan and non-political. "I enjoyed doing it and my readers seemed to like it. I wrote about the human interest side of a spouse's life. People have fantasies about the wonderful life a congressman's wife must lead. They think she luxuriates in beauty shops, saunas, and the like—in preparation for all the parties and balls. When, in truth, she's busy with housework, getting the children to the orthodontist, marketing, or bringing a clean shirt or change of underwear to the House for her husband." She laughs in animated humor.

It is quite true that this misconception flourishes even in the minds of the young wives who accompany their husbands to Washington. *The New York Times* recently reported on the kinds of lives these women lead. They may be wives of congressmen, heads of bureaus and departments, cabinet members, judges, presidential aides, or administrative assistants. Many give up a life that is promising for one that is strange and temporary. Some may abandon career plans. The majority exist in limbo. Their role is not clearly defined, so few know what is expected of them. A social life is practically non-existent. After an eighteen-hour day, a husband has neither time nor energy for dining out, bridge, or tennis. Even the cost of an evening out is prohibitive, if there are children to consider. Most of their friends are other lonely wives of the Washington circle. On weekends, they are alone because the husbands have returned to their districts. The wives console each other in their problems of loneliness, homesickness, and alienation.

The *Times* story reported an unhappy practice too. It related that it is not unusual for a father to only see his children asleep for weeks at a time. A wife gets a sleepy peck on the cheek in the morning and a tired one late at night. Even when they accompany their husbands to receptions, no one is particularly interested in them. They stand around with a frozen smile trying to look comfortable. The story made mention of the many who become disillusioned with this life of accommodation and return home. Others may ease the strain and pain with alcohol or transient affairs. One congressman's wife is reported to have found only one advantage to her status as his wife. "You get a place to park at the airport."

Mrs. Pettis, on the other hand, feels she had an advantage which equalled ten years experience when she embarked on the career of congresswoman. Involvement in her late husband's activities was more than adequate preparation. In addition, both had formed many longtime friendships on the Hill. She accompanied him to the district on weekends and often substituted for the congressman at speaking engagements. This helped her to become well known to the constitutents. "Oh, . . . how I miss those wonderful times," she says rather sadly. "They were very happy years. But now I do it alone."

In her brief career as a congresswoman, she has continued the work and interests of the late Representative Jerry L. Pettis. She speaks with fondness and pride about a bill conceived by her husband more than eight years ago. The California Desert Protection Bill is its title. "Because our vast California desert has been ravaged by people who steal priceless archeological artifacts and agricultural specimens as well as damage the top soil with off-road vehicles, something had to be done. There is a heritage represented out there that once destroyed can never be replaced. He felt in order to preserve the desert for future generations, we must have a program that will provide for the planned protection and development of this area. I worked very hard and finally was able to get the bill passed. People think of the desert as being arid and hearty. Actually it is a very fragile ecosystem."

Once the desert management plan is implemented, people will still be able to utilize specific roads and trails and enjoy the desert. They will do so in a responsible and coordinated manner.

Her bill provides for the development of a comprehensive long-range, multiple-use plan for the management, development, use, and protection of the California Desert. It has been incorporated into the Federal Land Policy and Management Act of 1976. "The California Desert Conservation Area Advisory Commission has been appointed by the Secretary of the Interior and I'm working very closely with the proceedings." Legislation she introduced to designate about 450,000 acres of land in the Joshua Tree National Monument as wilderness has also become a reality.

During Congresswoman Pettis' first term in office, she served on the Interior and Insular Affairs Committee and three of its subcommittees: Mines and Mining, Water and Power Resources, and Territorial and Insular Affairs—an assignment which was highly relevant to the problems of her district, an arid, rural area deeply concerned with the problems of land reclamation and energy. She was instrumental in the development of a program in conjunction with the Bureau of Reclamation—the Salton Sea Geothermal Complex Plan—to use saline water for the dual purpose of generating electrical power and facilitating irrigation.

With sixteen American Indian tribes in her district, Mrs. Pettis has also been active in matters involving the health and welfare of Indians. The Indian Health Services Bill contains some of her proposals.

A second campaign brought the congresswoman 71 percent of the vote and two new committee assignments: the House International Relations Committee and its Subcommittee on Europe and the Middle East; and the Education and Labor Committee and two of its subcommittees: Elementary, Secondary, and Vocational Education; and Labor-Management Relations.

"The history professor's daughter in me just won out," said Mrs. Pettis. "My first love has always been education, and the Education and Labor Committee assignment will allow me to concentrate a great deal of my efforts in several areas that are of particular importance to the 37th Congressional District."

A long and avid traveler and student of international relations, Mrs. Pettis vigorously sought a seat on the International Relations Committee. "I requested this committee assignment, because I feel that the Congress will be called upon more and more to oversee the direction of United States foreign policy. I want to make certain that the people of my district are well represented in any decision made in this vital area."

Congresswoman Pettis has two children, a son who is twenty-one years old and a daughter who is soon to be nineteen. "When they were little and there was so much to do, it was hard trying to raise them properly. I was fortunate because I always had domestic help. But more important, my family situation and relationships were warm and loving. My parents were very cooperative. For example, when my husband went to China in 1973 and I accompanied him, they supervised the care the children received. We were gone for three weeks, but I knew everything back home was in order so we had no worries. This kind of situation allowed me to be with my husband and really become an active partner in his career."

Mrs. Pettis believes there are certain characteristics one must have in order to be successful in public life. "If you don't really like people, don't go into politics or public office. If you're not concerned about people-related problems, politics is not for you. One must be flexible by nature, too. This job is not structured. Your reactions, at times, must be spontaneous. So you must be able to think on your feet. Too many things cannot be preconceived or planned in advance."

The congresswoman sees a bright future for women in public life. "In 1974, there were 630 women in state legislatures. We have eighteen women here now, but this will change. More and more women will become involved in government." She becomes very thoughtful and her brow wrinkles slightly. "One reason I say this is that women by nature are very compassionate. And we need compassion in this job. Sometimes I feel like a pastor with a parish of 550,000 people. I spend one weekend a month in my district 'ministering' to them. I think it's a great advantage to have been married and have children. This leads to some understanding of the problems with which people have to cope. And there are so many problems to be solved. We try, but we can't solve them all.

Many men are sensitive to problems and have compassion too. But a woman has to decide that she wants to work very hard. For some, it may not be worth it. And then, of course, you realize that you cannot please everyone. Your constituents, the press and columnists write about you . . . sometimes flattering things, other times they're critical. As for myself, one negative letter bothers me. No matter how insensitive I'd like to be, I can't be. That's my disposition! I do the best I can and all the other congresswomen do too. We're intemperate in our work habits . . . more so than men. We've got to learn how to be more restrained," she concludes.

Active in social, civic, and philanthropic work for many years, Congresswoman Pettis is a member of the California Elected Women's Association for Education and Research, the American Newspaper Women's Club, the National Women's Political Caucus—Republican Task Force, the California Board of Directors for the American Trauma Society, the Wednesday Group, the Environmental Study Conference, the American Historical Association, the Capitol Hill Club board of directors, and the Federal Employees' Association board of governors. She is also an outspoken member of the Congressional Women's Caucus.

There aren't too many free moments in her life. But when she finds the time, she reads and enjoys music. "I like all kinds—I'm an opera buff. I love the theater. The Kennedy Center has been sort of a lifeline for me, because I can lose myself completely in music and drama. I guess . . . because I'm a rancher, I love the out-of-doors and fresh air. I have this ranch that's high on the south slope of Mount Paloma— far, far away from everything and everyone. It's like an oasis. The peace and quiet are so relaxing. I don't get there often, but when I do the environment is refreshing for body and soul." Her face reflects the sense of contentment that she derives from those too infrequent visits.

Mrs. Pettis reveals some of her inner strength and fortitude through this story. "I had to decide upon my candidacy within a week of my husband's death. It was a very difficult decision to make in such an emotional state. There would be twelve opponents. They said, 'she's not tough enough to do the job.' So all over the district, 27,000 square miles, I debated these twelve men on every issue. But the question of 'toughness' persisted. So one day, I said, 'No I'm not tough, but I'm strong.' No one expected me to get anywhere near 50 percent of the vote. There would be a runoff for sure, they predicted. But I surprised them by winning 60 percent of the vote."

Congresswoman Pettis didn't have the full support of her children at first. "My son was nineteen at the time. Peter was bitter and angry that his Daddy worked so hard and was so tired. He felt this physical condition attributed to the plane crash. My husband was a competent pilot with over 18,000 hours of flying. And he crashed in an area that he knew like the back of his hand! Peter knew that his father had recently concluded a successful campaign and was tired, and should not have been conducting such an exhausting schedule in his district. But Jerry Pettis was not only an able congressman but an outstanding statesman. He was totally devoted to his job. Peter said, 'Mother, we have given enough. We don't need the money and we don't need the job.' But Debbie, my daughter, said, 'Mother, I know how much you loved working with Dad and how much it meant for you to be with him. You're important to the people in the district. They love you. I know how you feel. Dad was the first Republican to hold that seat. And you are the only one who could begin to replace him. And if you want to do it, do it! You'll be unhappy just running the ranch. So do it!' She was just sixteen . . . going on sixty. She had such insight. So I faced this split within my own family." Congresswoman Pettis takes a deep breath and continues with a smile. "Now Peter is a pilot and has been flying a year with Alaskan Central Airlines. And that really took some important decision-making after what happened to his father. I remember that after I'd been in office for about a year, he visited me in Washington. He followed me around for about a week, but he didn't have much to say. Then toward the end of the week, he put his arms around me and said, 'Mom, I just couldn't be more proud of you.'"

Mrs. Pettis plans to remain in public life. She loves the House, and is not interested in a state job. She is not a feminist activist, but believes that everyone should have opportunities and alternatives—men and women. There are millions of people who need to have this point of view expressed and represented. The congresswoman represents them well.

Patricia S. Schroeder

Although the appointment was an early one, 9:00 A.M., Representative Schroeder's day had begun much earlier. She arrived about thirty minutes late because of a committee meeting and House business. It is obvious that, to her, being a congresswoman is a great responsibility.

"I never really thought of entering public life until about four weeks before I announced my candidacy," she explains. But in 1972, being thirty-one and the mother of two small children, her declaration surprised many people. "My husband, Jim, was much more interested in politics than I was. They were looking for a candidate and couldn't find one." So her husband convinced her to run for Congress. Being part-time lawyer and housewife didn't seem like much preparation for the job. But Congresswoman Schroeder says, "Now I don't think there are any particular personal characteristics that you can identify that really make you effective on the job. This is a job that requires a very broad background. A law degree isn't essential. It's the ability to think, to be creative and

185

tenacious. You mustn't be afraid to compete. Formal academic preparation is not that important."

For any woman, running for public office is difficult. But for a young mother, it appeared impossible. The Democratic powers of Denver would not accept Pat Schroeder as a viable candidate. She couldn't expect support from organized labor either. But she didn't give in to the pressures and rejections. Older and respected opinion-makers wanted her to be rather neutral. But Pat Schroeder is a fighter and compromise is alien to her nature. She opposed the Vietnam War and said so. She was against the state's plan to host the 1976 Winter Olympics, and she let her views be known. "Neither the environment nor the taxpayers could afford such an extravaganza," she argued. Using nontraditional tactics of posing without family and confronting issues, Pat Schroeder won the Democratic Party nomination by a comfortable margin. She drew large crowds to her speeches and, utimately, to the polls. In the general election, she won over the incumbent by 8,000 votes.

Making the roles of wife, mother and congresswoman compatible and successful is no easy trick. Pat Schroeder is the first to admit it. "There are days when I almost don't manage," she laughs heartily. "It is not an easy life. We have someone who cares for the children during the day. They're now ten- and six-years-old and live here with us," she expands. "Seeing them and being with them every day is ideal, of course. But one must remember, as a woman you have an entirely different commitment than that of a man. Because so many men still have wives who deal with all the garbage, this continues to be a fact of life. But my husband has a career, and he can't do the mundane, everyday things. And it really is a strain. I wouldn't tell anyone that this life is a great 'fun trip,'" she states flatly. "One is always putting priorities in order. You just have to decide what you want to be the most. And just how selfifish you are, too—because if you need time for yourself, you'd better forget it!

"I don't have any special hobbies or interests," Mrs. Schroeder says, "because there's just no time. When I have a minute I read, because, no matter how hard you work, you're always so far behind. The planning on general purposes, the army issues—all of this becomes my reading matter." She gestures toward an old, large desk that's practically covered with mail, manila envelopes, documents, and folders.

Congresswoman Schroeder is one of two female members of the House Armed Services Committee. As an avid supporter of equal rights for women, she fought for admission of women to West Point. She is not warmly welcomed by the majority of men who deal with the issues of huge war ships and aircraft, militia, five-star generals, and bombers. This is truly the forte of the most ultramasculine, or so the male members would like to believe. She fights, almost alone, for reduced spending on military matters. The congresswoman would prefer to see these huge sums of money diverted to day care, food stamps, and education. These are the concerns, she feels, that relate to constituents' needs everywhere.

As are most congresswomen, she is appalled by what might be called a lack of ethics and morality among some members of Congress. Lobbyists are constantly showering everyone with gifts to help win legislation favorable to their causes, but the women are not so easily tempted. Of course, double standards in other behavior exist, too. A congresswoman has to be careful with whom she's seen and where. Petty gossip can diminish one's integrity and image for constituents back home.

Since Watergate, there has been a demand for "clean government." Whether this degree of political purity is within human reach is debatable. At the moment, moralistic fervor is in full swing among the new appointees of the Carter administration. Since, in many people's minds, there is a direct connection between permitting a private citizen to pay for one's lunch, golf fees, or airline ticket, congressional votes and views must be above censure. Congresswoman Schroeder has had her share of attempted inducement, including everything from twenty-five pounds of cheese to a mink coat.

Pat Schroeder ponders the question of job and personal satisfaction to be gained by members of Congress. She says with a feeling of honesty and sincerity, ringed with cynicism, "I'm not really sure. It's a very tenuous thing. If you're in public life, you have to be very thickskinned, especially if you're a woman or a minority group member. You're just a living, moving target twenty-four hours a day. And you really have to be prepared to take that. As for real satisfaction, I'm not so sure. What we do here is so esoteric. You are one of 435 members. You cast a vote. And rarely does anything win by one vote. Rarely is a speech given that turns everyone around. It just doesn't happen. It's all set in cement. Most people know the movie version," she explains with a deep sigh.

In response to the question of bills sponsored by the congresswoman that make her proud, she explains, "There are about 17,000 bills introduced each year. And I've introduced quite a few. But most of them that I'm proud of or really liked —never got passed." She flashes a sardonic grin. "Because they're not ready for them yet, I guess. You get a little discouraged." However, she continues to press for change through her membership on the House Post Office and Civil Service Committee and by being chairwoman of its Subcommittee on Employee Ethics and Utilization.

Pat Schroeder has no aspirations for higher office. She'll keep hoping and working toward citizens' gains made possible by legislation passed in Congress. "This will be my contribution." Her family life is a happy one, though sometimes hectic. Her children, Scott and Jamie, are as "normal" as any other bright, healthy children their ages. "It's hard to plan ahead, because you never know who's going to be in town. The children view life as having both good and bad parts. The bad part is the frequent absence of parents." But with two incomes, the Schroeders can afford to take the children with them when they travel or tour. This is the good part. "I would say—the irregular hours we have are the worst part. I just hope and pray that the good and bad balance each other out. But then again you never know," she ends wistfully.

Jim and Pat Schroeder met and married while attending Harvard Law School. From the onset, both agreed to follow careers. This early planning probably accounts for, at least in part, their harmonious relationship. He is associated with a Washington-based international law firm. A flexible work schedule permits him to enjoy recreational and other occasions with his children. Both parents try very hard to maintain, as nearly as possible, a regularly paced home environment. The children seem to thrive. They don't view their home life as being unusual, because it's always been this way. As frequently as possible, Pat Schroeder has an early breakfast with her children, and may even see them during the day or talk with them by telephone. Her husband plans similar contacts. "People seem to be amazed that Jim Schroeder is so well adjusted and content with his life style. They don't realize that there's a difference between the spouses of congressmen and congresswomen. A congressman can send his wife in his place to half of the teas, tape cuttings, and openings. His wife often makes the speech, when there is a conflict in his schedule. But a congresswoman's husband doesn't do any of these things. I have to go everywhere. But, of course, I wouldn't want him to anyway. So he doesn't have that political spouse role!"

Jim Schroeder gave Pat the greatest amount of encouragement and support for this arduous job, along with a group of supportive friends. However, her friends have more difficulty in dealing with public criticism about her than Pat does. "They are very protective and clearly open-ended," she says warmly.

Although she hasn't patterned her life style after anyone, Congresswoman Schroeder admired Eleanor Roosevelt. "I'm hoping to see more women in responsible roles, but I'm quite discouraged at this stage. In 1964, there were twenty-one women in the House and now there's only eighteen. We should be gaining instead of losing. In thirteen years we've lost three. The highwater mark was twenty. I hope women will continue to persevere. But, in addition to special personal character-istics, one also needs to get money. And for women to raise large sums of money is an almost impossible task. If we ever get public funding, that would certainly help. It's really amazing. Just the entry fee is between $150,000 and $200,000. How many people can afford that or are able to raise it? Men can do it with all their friends—all trading checks."

Journalists and others are concerned that distinguished and able men and women are increasingly reluctant to enter politics. It would be tragic if only those who are financially able can be the only candidates. Of course, Congresswoman Schroeder hopes that there will be some public support for candidates in the near future. "We saw this in the presidential race. But even partial support would help a great deal."

The congresswoman certainly keeps well within her budget. Her office is spartan. She has small quarters. Her staff is used most effectively. She doesn't send any weekly or monthly newsletters back to the district. "I keep in touch with my sup-porters through my regular visits. My time schedule is pub-licized, and the people know when and where to see me. It's very hard, but I do keep within my budget."

One of Congresswoman Schroeder's great joys is her chil-dren. She laughingly tells of how frequently reporters want to interview them. Then they are disappointed, because the children are so normal. "Well—they don't know any other kind of life. There's nothing so unique about our life. They're like kids of working parents everywhere," she chuckles. "They have no hang-ups because their mother works. She has always worked."

Pat Schroeder has a brother who practices law in Denver. There are three lawyers within the family, and there may be more some day. Her children continue to grow and develop healthy and positive attitudes. Raising them and working a fourteen-hour day is not easy. The demands of her office are, at times, overwhelming, but as she recently told the press, "I would say that most of the women who are qualified to be congresswomen have dealt with this issue all of their lives." Her husband's life has been enriched too, because the Schroeders have functioned as a family unit with respect, recognition, and acceptance of each other's talents. Congresswoman Pat Schroeder is very much a part of her time.

Virginia Smith

Today my appointment schedule is meaningless. The House is in session and every member of Congress is participating or interested in the heated discussion taking place on the floor. The issue concerns picketing by unions that would stop all work at construction sites. Tomorrow's newspapers will report the defeat of the proposal. I must wait until Congresswoman Smith has an opportunity to leave the floor. I decide to follow a group of tourists into Statuary Hall. Legislation in 1864 created this National Statuary Hall out of the Old Hall, the chamber of the House from 1807 to 1857. It was designed by Benjamin Henry Latrobe (1764–1820) in 1815. Mr. Latrobe was a famous architect who introduced the use of Greek forms in public buildings. His Bank of the United States, now the old Philadelphia Custom House, was based on the Parthenon. In 1805, he built the first American cathedral, the Roman Catholic Cathedral in Baltimore. He also designed Sedgely (1800), a residence near Philadelphia, as an example of Gothic-revival in America.

Within this beautiful ninety-six foot semicircular, domed

rotunda with massive marble columns and a graceful balcony, there are bronze and marble statues. All the states were invited to provide and furnish not more than two statues of deceased persons who have rendered distinguished civic or military services. Because of the great weight, this magnificent room contains only one statue from each of the fifty states. The other statues are in different locations in the Capitol.

As I stroll around with tourists and guides, I see many well-known names. Statues of Will Rogers of Oklahoma, Brigham Young of Utah, Jefferson Davis of Mississippi, Robert Fulton of Pennsylvania, Sam Houston of Texas, and Robert Lee of Virginia are here. The guides are pointing out others like Kamehameha I—the First King of all Hawaii—William Jennings Bryan of Nebraska, Henry Clay of Kentucky, and Daniel Webster of New Hampshire.

Objects of art and paintings of artistic merit and sentimental significance have become national heirlooms in the Capitol building. The Capitol collection today conissts of some 681 works of art. There are, for example, 124 portraits of presidents, vice presidents, speakers, senators, chairmen of the House Committee on Appropriations, architects of the Capitol, and other men and women of prominence in history. There are fifty-three paintings other than portraits and eighty marble and bronze busts. There are nine statues other than those contributed by states for the Statuary Hall collection.

"Oh, there you are." I turned at the sound of the cheerful voice. Congresswoman Smith was responding to my page. She had found it possible to leave the floor and meet with me. Her spontaneous smile was like a refreshing breeze on a hot humid day. "Let's find a quiet spot," she whispered.

Mrs. Smith's grooming for the position of congresswoman was rather subtle and unintentional. Born in Randolph, Iowa, she attended Iowa public schools. Her mother was a former school teacher who supplemented her formal education with lessons at home. "I remember when I was a little girl, we had this blackboard in the dining room. And every day, my mother printed a new word on it. The goal was to increase my vocabulary by 1000 words in three years. We were of modest circumstances. I am proud to say that I wore hand-me-downs—adult clothes cut down to my size. My dolls were often pictures cut out of catalogues. My folks worked hard and long on the farm. So my background included the good old Protestant work ethic! And even today, I am being compensated by that early enrichment in my life."

Before coming to Washington, she was active in her local community and throughout the state of Nebraska. A graduate of the University of Nebraska, Mrs. Smith served on the Nebraska State Board of Education for ten years. She was the first and only woman to have that honor. She also was elected national chairman of the Farm Bureau Women, and served in that position for twenty years. She worked arduously with young people in 4H Clubs, and has received the National 4H Alumni Award. She served as the national chairman of the Rural Development Commission. The National Commission for Community Health Service was another interest, and Mrs. Smith was appointed to serve on the commission for six years. "So you see, all of these interests and committee assignments were preparing and broadening me for a greater role in public life," she reasons. She was active in the Republican Party, too. "I was county chairman and the state vice chairman of Founder's Day. My church work brought me into contact with local groups, too. I was a Sunday school teacher for seventeen years.

When the congressional representative from her district decided not to run again, Mrs. Smith received numerous telephone calls from people who were aware of her extensive service record. She had demonstrated a deep interest in people and people-related concerns. The callers suggested that she run for Congress. After discussing the matter thoroughly with Haven, her husband, they decided on New Year's Day 1974 that she should be a candidate. "We had never elected a woman to Congress, so this was a new idea for Nebraskans. There were ten candidates—nine nice young men and me. I was elected by a narrow margin in 1974—the first time . . . but by a greater plurality (74 percent) in 1976," she beams. "One important aspect of my first victory was the help I received from the six young men I defeated in the primary. There was no bitterness. They recognized and accepted me as the people's choice and worked hard to help me win in the general election. My winning will help citzens appraise future candidates' qualifications rather than the gender. Other women will have greater opportunity for victory in Nebraska now," Mrs. Smith says as she flashes that brilliant smile which she projects so naturally and easily.

Congresswoman Smith finds the other members' response to her gratifying. "When you rise to speak, no one is concerned with the sex of the speaker. The members study your philosophy, ability, and dedication. Men and women are given equal consideration. I think more doors are opening up to women who have the qualification to do the job."

Like all other congresswomen, Mrs. Smith finds her job tremendously challenging but rewarding. "I love this career. I just love it!" she exclaims enthusiastically. "I've worked all of my life . . . worked very hard—so I don't think I'm working any harder now. It's just that I'm working on different things. I don't see any negative aspects to this career from my viewpoint. If I were a young family man, I could see real problems in achieving satisfaction and a happy family life. This would be difficult. A member of Congress returns to the district to work on weekends. If there are very young children, the wife must remain in Washington with them. If there are school-age children, there are other decisions to be made regarding taking the family away from or to Washington. So for young people, male or female, political life is so demanding that it is hard to maintain a satisfactory family life. But it can be done and many members of Congress are achieving success in their personal lives as well as in their public ones." Mrs. Smith pauses to reflect. "There are some good things about entering a political career at a later time in life. For instance, my husband is here with me. We have an apartment. It's just the two of us—we have no children to worry about. So he helps me just as a wife would assist her congressman husband. Today we had guests from the 3rd District. So when I had to go to the floor, he finished lunching with them and then took them on a tour of the Capitol. Often he takes people to the airport. He does many of the things a congressman's wife would do. Of course, the best part is that he loves it!"

Perhaps one of the reasons for this union's success lies in the similarity of backgrounds. "Haven graduated from the University of Nebraska, too, and is a wheat rancher. We were married when I was nineteen and still in college. We had no assets, but a whole lot of love. He came from a ranch family just like I came from a family engaged in farming. We are not lawyers, but both of us earned a bachelor's degree. My husband has a great deal of dedication and concern for grass-roots issues, too. He goes home with me every weekend. Our car has been driven more than 30,000 miles this past year in the district alone. We do everything together." Her face is mirrored with a sense of contentment.

To keep her constituents informed of her activities and voting record, Congresswoman Smith sends a box-holder newsletter to Nebraskans four times a year. Early in January 1977, the congresswoman introduced a bill to remove a provision from the estate tax law which would be a burden to all farmers and small business. Nationwide, family-owned and operated farms number three million, so this legislation is important to land owners everywhere. This is just one example of how the congresswoman's efforts in Washington assist the folks back home.

Another time, Representative Smith voiced concern about rural post offices. In land size, her congressional district comprises about three-fourths of the state of Nebraska. The cities and towns, generally, are small and far apart. In some counties, there are only three or four communities. Many of the people live on farms and ranches, and earn their living from the land. For them, mail is one of the primary means of contact with the outside world. Although telephone communications and road systems have improved over the years in rural America, the delivery of the mail has always—and will continue to be—something special and symbolic. Small towns depend greatly upon the post office for their identity. The *Congressional Record* of February 2, 1977, printed Representative Smith's testimony. Among other things she said, "I ask that you please remember the public service responsibilities of the postal service when you (the Commission) make your recommendations. We all want to make the postal service operate as effectively as possible, but we also must ensure that all Americans—whether they live in Los Angeles, Chicago, Topeka, Lincoln, or Tryon, Nebraska—have equal access to the services provided.

"The frustration of those who feel because they live in a farm area and are not getting equal treatment is typified by a letter I recently received from a constituent who gets his mail delivered three days a week, but must come to town to pick it up the other three days.

"He writes: 'I can get by with three day deliveries, but I don't really like it. I pay the same for stamps as most other people, but only get half the service.' "

Congresswoman Smith also let her supporters and constituents know how she felt about United States' aid to India.

"The International Development Association, in 1976 alone, provided India with 42 percent of the IDA budget, which amounts to $627 million. And most of their loans have been of the so-called 'soft' variety, meaning India has up to fifty years to repay at interest rates of 1 to 3 percent," the congresswoman reported. She also noted that India has been openly hostile to the United States, even though we are the largest contributor to the IDA. India also maintains close military collaboration with the Soviet Union, and is the only country in the world licensed to manufacture the Russian MIG 21 fighter airplane.

Congresswoman Smith spoke out against plans of the Missouri River Division of the Army Corps of Engineers. A regulatory program to dredge and fill would extend to all of Nebraska's twenty-two rivers and most of its streams at the cost of $340,000 during one fiscal year. She found this plan untenable and introduced legislation to limit the corps to waters which are presently used, or are susceptible to use in their natural condition or by reasonable improvement as a means to transport interstate or foreign commerce.

She is beginning her second term, but her committee participation is impressive: the Committee on Education and Labor and its Subcommittees on Manpower, Compensation and Health and Safety, and Post-Secondary Education; the Interior and Insular Affairs Committee, and Subcommittees on National Parks and Recreation, Water and Power Resources; and the House Republican Task Force on Committee Reform.

Representative Smith has introduced bills which would protect the confidentiality of an individual's bank records against the intrusion of a government agency. Her bill would establish a program of congressional review in this area, ensuring that all new government regulations be submitted to Congress.

She currently serves on the Committee on Appropriations.

Subcommittee assignments include Foreign Operations and Public Works. She is a member of the Republican Policy Committee, too.

The congresswoman could be your next-door neighbor, the Scout den mother, or your favorite hospital volunteer. She is natural and unpretentious. One can almost imagine her knowing hundreds of thousands of her constituents by their first names. When she speaks of her commitment, her eyes burn brightly.

To young women interested in politics, she advises that a willingness to work hard is mandatory. "If you want to do a good job, you've got to work hard. One must study all the issues, read, make telephone calls, hold conferences, and do research. The vote is number one! Then the people back home have problems which need your ear. Good health is important too. One needs endless amounts of energy." Mrs. Smith shifts slightly in her chair and looks directly into my eyes. "You have to have the courage of your convictions. If you really believe in your position, then you can't be swayed. You must vote as you see it. It will always be a risk, but you must be willing to stand up and be counted," Mrs. Smith sums up.

"Congress needs people who are representative of all groups of citizens in our country. They should be men and women from everywhere. Each has a unique viewpoint which is essential to making our country work." The congresswoman doesn't concern herself solely with what might be called "women's issues." "I've always believed that every problem is a woman's problem as well as a man's problem. For example—inflation is a woman's problem. Who buys the food and children's clothes? Agricultural policy affects a woman. Will she get a good steak in the market, and how much will it cost? What about sugar? Do we drive our sugar producers out of business and then have to resort to imports which drive the price tag sky high? So all issues involve women and men."

This energetic and dedicated public servant plans to return to Congress as often and for as long as her supporters want her. When there is time, Mrs. Smith enjoys reading. The Smiths are homebodies and not party-goers. They attend church services every Sunday wherever they happen to be. Although members of the Methodist church, they visit churches of all faiths.

"Twenty years from now, there will be little differences between opportunities for men and women. I'm certain because, when you look back, we've come so far so fast. The message is loud and clear all across the country. Women will have equal rights in every aspect of their lives. These rights will free men, too, because women will sense the magnitude of being a wife and a mother. The pendulum will swing back to more closely-knit family life. I think everyone is aware of the drugs, crime, and other related problems among our youth. But changes are being seen and cohesiveness in family relations will help reduce these problems."

Mrs. Smith recalls an incident which occurred when she was just fifteen-years-old and a recent high school graduate. "I was expecting to have my first date. And, of course, I was terribly excited, My sweet, little old grandmother gave me this advice. 'Now Virginia—you just don't pay any attention to boys! You just study your lessons. And one day you'll go to Congress, and you'll meet a real man!' Congress was certainly not on my agenda, but the young man was. But my grandmother must have had some intuition, because part of her prophecy came true. I did come to Congress, but I brought my real man with me."

Gladys Noon Spellman

Most people know that one of the greatest assets of a good teacher is the ability to recognize and meet the needs of students. Gladys Spellman was such a teacher. Yet, Mrs. Spellman's sensitivities extended beyond the classroom and into the community. She observed that a great many citizens' needs were not being met. Although Mrs. Spellman was involved in civic activities, others recognized in her the potential for extending that talent into greater dimensions. Friends urged her to run for county commissioner, even though no woman had ever been elected to that position. She ran and led the ticket. Campaigning costs were nominal. "I think my expenditures were about $35.00," she recalls. "And it was a county-wide campaign in a county with a population of more than 600,000 people. Of special significance was the fact that my election proved that a woman could run and be successful."

Like her colleagues, Congresswoman Spellman confirms that being a woman merely interested in politics is insufficient background for public life. "If a woman has been active, made a name for herself, and has the respect of community groups, people will support her. They can then relate to her, because they know she believes in them, their convictions." The congresswoman relaxes and then adds. "They must feel that if she's elected, things will change!" After her initial success as a member of the board of county commissioners of Prince George County in 1962, Mrs. Spellman was re-elected in 1966 and later served as board chairman.

In 1967, Mrs. Spellman was appointed by President Johnson to the Advisory Commission on Intergovernmental Relations. When her county adopted its charter in 1971, she was elected to the council-at-large. There are over 3,000 counties in the United States, and, in 1972, she was elected president of the National Association of Counties. Mrs. Spellman is the only woman ever to have been elected to that position. "It was most unusual. Because most county leaders consider the presidency a prize, there is vigorous campaigning by the candidates and state supporters. I'd never even thought about the position seriously. And to my surprise, I discovered seven state organizations had nominated me." Mrs. Spellman smiles, remembering. "My being a woman was a slight advantage because I was clearly visible in a crowd of men. But in all candor, I had proved my ability to do the job. And that's what called attention to me."

No one says that making it in the political world is easy. "But women need to know that it can be done. Women can be elected. But it's a tougher road, because it isn't easy to raise money. Men make larger contributions to campaigns; generally, women don't. Women contribute five and ten dollars, but men contribute thousands of dollars. So a female candidate can have a disadvantage. But if a woman is known and her capacity for leadership is recognized by both men and women, then she just doesn't need large sums of money." Mrs. Spellman's advice stems from her broad background of governmental and civic posts at the national, state, and local levels.

We are sitting at the table in the kitchen of the Congressional Women's Lounge. It is very quiet here, but the hallways and stairs are noisy with many tourists, aides, and congressional members moving about. Some are rushing to or from committee meetings or receptions, others are being interviewed by the press, and many are standing around in small groups discussing important bills and issues. Congresswoman Spellman has taken a few minutes out of her own committee meeting to express her views. She glances at her watch and continues.

"Just recently I met a young woman who works here in the Congress and who intends to run for Congress in her district. She's a bright individual and probably knows the legislation and the issues as well as anybody. But she isn't going to get elected, and she doesn't understand what's wrong. The fact is—she has no base! She hasn't done anything back home or achieved any recognition. The mere fact that she works on the Hill doesn't mean a thing to her constituents. What they want is someone to whom they can relate, and then the issues will fall into place. It's the image that your constituents have of you that's so important!" she states with feeling.

Congresswoman Spellman points out that a woman's point of view differs from that held by a man. This is one reason why women are so needed in the Congress and other areas of political life. "Women think, for the most part, in terms of the individual . . . the person. We know the individual bleeds, hurts, has pains and aches, and many problems. Men think in terms of totals. So that balance of thinking is important."

The congresswoman loves her work. She was fortunate enough to have found her direction early. But she advises girls to begin their preparation for a political career as early as high school. They should start moving in that direction and leave nothing to chance. Women must be prepared. Preparation means studying and learning about politics. "And, politics ought to be the most honorable word in our language—standing right there beside motherhood and apple pie!" she says in a stern voice that's modified by a gentle laugh. "And politics can be honorable, if we get the right people involved. People who are there because they want to accomplish things for others make the field respectable. We don't need people who are selfishly building up their own egos and empires. Women can help bring about that kind of change."

Because of her first profession, teaching, Mrs. Spellman presents guidance in a systematic and orderly way. "Girls need to know history, political science, and economics. They should involve themselves in their communities by doing volunteer work in all areas. Even as young women, they can begin to start doing things that bring about change in their communities. And soon residents will perceive them as 'doers' and the kind of people they want to have represent them."

Congresswoman Spellman has managed a happy family life of children and politics. Her children were young teenagers when she began her political career. As a family, all the members played active roles in community life prior to that time. Her children grew up with a sense of doing and giving as part of the family life style. As a result, she thinks they're much more interesting people. "They learned to be self-sufficient and work well together. Of course—I don't hesitate to tell you that I do my own housework today. And often while I'm talking on the telephone at 7:00 A.M., I'm holding a mop in the other hand. There's work to be done at home, too." She laughs gaily visualizing this non-public image. "I have a most marvelous husband, and I give him an enormous amount of the credit." The congresswoman's voice grows gentle and serious, "While many of the women don't like to say that husbands are important, I have to admit that if I didn't have the right kind of climate, . . . I would have chosen my marriage rather than political life." Mrs.

Spellman's face wears a glorious smile which mirrors a deeper happiness. "He's an engineer, but retired now. But he's a mature and secure man in his own right, so he was never threatened by my endeavors. That's so important to know! His manhood was never in jeopardy, so he helped wash the dishes and clothes, made beds, and assisted with the cooking. But I do those same things, too, although I have a career. We've had a really wonderful life. He has his talents and his arena. What I do better, I do. And what he does well, he enjoys. I never insist that he appear with me at meetings. If it is something that might interest him or I need him, he'll accompany me. He recently turned down a television show, because he thought that I'd be more suited for that." She gave a warm and sudden smile. "This all means, of course, that when we're together, we have so much to talk about and share."

Congresswoman Spellman calls herself a workaholic. Reading her biography leads one to believe that there might be some reason for her feeling that way. She has served on the National Labor-Management Relations Service, the Steering Committee of the Urban Affairs Committee of the National Council of State Governments, the Board of Directors of the National Association of Regional Councils, and the Democratic Advisory Committee of Elected Officials.

At the state level, she has been a member of the Governor's Commission on Law Enforcement and the Administration of Justice, the Governor's Commission to Determine the State's Role in Financing Public Education, chairman of the Maryland State Comprehensive Health Planning Advisory Council, and board member and education committee chairman of the Maryland Association of Counties.

At the regional level, she chaired the Washington Suburban Transit Commission, and was chairman of Regional Planning Board IV created by the Federal Omnibus Crime Control and Safe Streets Act, board member of the Washington Metropolitan Area Transit Authority, and vice–president of the Metropolitan Washington Council of Governments.

She has also served on many county boards, including welfare, library, mental health, family service, Red Cross and cerebral palsy. For eight years, she was chairman of the Prince George's County General Hospital board of trustees.

Representative Gladys Noon Spellman, Democratic congresswoman from the 5th District of Maryland, was elected to the United States House of Representatives on November 7, 1974. As vice chairman of the group of seventy-five newly elected Democrats, she played a leadership role in the reform of House rules and procedures. One of the major changes brought about was the dismantling of the seniority system in the selection of committee chairpersons. Congresswoman Spellman was assigned to the Committee on Banking, Currency, and Housing and to the Committee on Post Office and Civil Service, both of which will consider legislation of vital importance to people of the 5th District.

"My hobbies are my grandchildren. I have delightful ones. My daughter Dana is twenty-eight with two children, Rick is thirty, and Steven, my oldest, is thirty-two. He has two children. Our days and nights are so full here that every free minute is valued. I remember once I had an hour and ten minutes between meetings. I told my husband, Reuben, that I planned to race over to Dana's house. He said, 'You're out of your mind. It will take an hour in travel time and you'll only have ten minutes left!' 'Well, I'll spend those ten minutes with my grandsons.' So I got into the car and sped over to Dana's house. She had just put little Brandy to bed. But she went upstairs and brought him down. He was just a toddler then—about two years old. I hid in the family room. My daughter said, 'Brandy go find Nana.' He tottered into the hallway and looked all around. 'Go ahead, honey look for Nana,' Dana urged. Brandy looked puzzled for a minute, and then ran into the room, turned on the television set and sat down to wait for Nana. Dana and I both enjoyed this delightful incident."

Mrs. Spellman radiates a spirit of warmth and benevolence that grows out of a highly developed sense of values. She has passed these precepts on to her children and grandchildren. She reveals a recent incident involving her eight-year-old grandson, Heath.

On a recent visit to the House, he was impressed by the number of people who recognized and spoke to his grandmother, the congresswoman. Heath said, "Nan . . . you're very important." I replied. 'Indeed I am. Do you know why I'm important?' And he said, "Because you're a member of Congress." 'Yes, I am. But that's not what makes me important. I'm important, because I'm a human being and all human beings are important.' He looked up at me and replied in a voice tinged with disdain. "Well . . . I don't think so." 'Well —let's think about it honey. Would you say that a garbage man is important?' "Of course not!" 'Well, then suppose all the garbage men in the country went on strike during the hot summer months. The garbage piled up, the smell was awful, flies were everywhere, and disease began to spread in every city. Who do you think your neighbors would prefer to have come and help out—the congresswoman—or the garbage man?' Health thought for a moment. "Oh, the garbage man!" 'Well you see everyone is important . . . everyone has some contribution to make.'

That evening, I was conversing with someone and my guest looked down at Heath and said, 'Young man . . . you know your grandmother is a very important person!' Heath looked up at him with saucer-like eyes and said, "Yes. And so is the garbage man."

Leonor K. Sullivan

Born and raised in St. Louis, Missouri, Leonor Kretzer Sullivan is among that group of congresswomen who filled a seat in Congress formerly held by their deceased husbands. More than a third of Congresswomen have served in this way. But the widow of Representative John Berchmans Sullivan did not automatically get his seat. She had to lead her own fight to get the Democratic nomination. Despite the fact that voters knew and remembered her as one of the first women to join her husband on the campaign trail, party leaders considered her a non-vote-getter. No primary is held in special elections to fill vacancies caused by death or resignation. The chairmen of the congressional district of the major parties select the candidate to be the nominee. When the chairman of the 3rd Congressional District met with the award leaders to select a nominee for the democrats to fill the vacancy caused by Congressman Sullivan's death, they did not name Leonor Sullivan. They said, "Leonor, we have nothing against you as a person, but we want to win this special election. And a woman cannot win in Missouri." So they named a state legislator—a male—as the nominee. With their *man*, the Democrats lost the election. After this, Mrs. Sullivan felt that she had to show up the party's blind spot toward women.

Mrs. Sullivan returned to Washington and worked for a year to earn the money necessary to conduct her own primary fight. She was victorious without the Democratic Party's support. In fact, Mrs. Sullivan defeated the Republican who had won the previous year in the special election by 50,000 votes. Mrs. Sullivan recalls, "Since I had spent nearly ten years working with my husband, I thought it would be better to pursue work in the government rather than return to my previous business connections."

It isn't difficult to understand a widow's desire to carry out her husband's ambitions. In many cases, however, these desires are honorable and laudable, but unrealistic. There are some exceptions, like Mrs. Sullivan. Senator Margaret Chase Smith of Maine, Representative Edith Nourse Rogers of Massachusetts, and Frances P. Bolton of Ohio are notable, but most of these women are rarely heard from once they've served out their deceased husbands' terms.

With Congresswoman Sullivan's election, the number of females in the 83rd Congress (1953-55) rose to twelve. This number included the veteran Senator Margaret Chase Smith and two fellow Republicans from Nebraska, Eva Bowring and Hazel H. Abel. Mrs. Bowring filled the vacancy created by the death of Senator Dwight Griswold while Mrs. Abel served sixty days of an unexpired term. (Nebraska has a state law stipulating that an appointee may serve only "until the next regular election" and that a candidate seeking the six-year term may not run for the two remaining months of unexpired term.)

As a freshman congresswoman, Mrs. Sullivan was assigned to the Merchant Marine and Fisheries Committee. This was just the beginning of a fruitful and rewarding political career in the House that lasted twenty-four years. She smiles as she remembers her reluctance to even marry a politician. She says, "Back in my courting days, it was difficult for me to decide to marry a man who was in politics. My husband-to-be was a lawyer, but he was in politics. I told him that I'd marry him tomorrow, if he went back to his law practice and got out of politics. Well, he didn't do it! And I'm glad he didn't. He taught me how wrong I was. His argument was, 'We have one of the best and enduring forms of government, and it can only continue to be so if good, honest, and dedicated people offer themselves to be elected to office.' "

Congresswoman Sullivan's record is long and rich. In 1955, while still a member of the Merchant Marine Committee, she was also elected to the House Banking and Currency Committee. Under that committee, she was also appointed to serve on the Housing Subcommittee. From 1957 to 1971, Congresswoman Sullivan was chairman of the Subcommittee on Panama Canal which functionos under the Merchant Marine and Fisheries Committee. During this period, she directed numerous stuides into the operational problems and activities of the Panama Canal Company. She opposed treaty proposals to cede the Canal Zone and the Panama Canal to the Republic of Panama. The Subcommittee on Merchant Marine and Coast Guard, among others, profited by her membership.

"One of the best ways to be effective in Congress," she observes, "is to concentrate your abilities on one or two areas. Over the years, I've discovered that the best techniques that make for effectiveness come from doing your homework. I've found it most helpful not to co-sponsor or support every piece of legislation introduced in the House. One cannot know everything about all subjects, but, through the years, I've tried to choose and sponsor and then support certain legislation and causes. These would be issues beneficial to my constituency or those issues I believed to be in the best interest of the nation as a whole."

To illustrate this principle, she spent an enormous amount

of personal energy and effort in two areas. One dealt with consumer buying. Congresswoman Sullivan researched, studied, and learned everything possible about laws and regulations dealing with buying on credit. She was determined that consumers know the truth about the cost of credit—the true annual rates of interest charged by those companies extending credit to their customers. This knowledge would permit buyers to comparison-shop for the best credit value available. At hearings, she spoke out against practices of retail stores and mail-order houses hiding the true cost of using credit. The congresswoman approved of buying on credit, if one knew how to handle credit. However, she felt that it was imperative that the public know the true annual rate being charged for the use of credit—just as they know the annual rate they are paid by banks or other financial institutions on their saving accounts. She felt that if the average citizen knew the real cost of credit, he could use it more wisely and not overextend his ability to pay debts. Her enthusiasm for the task came to the attention of President Johnson who assigned her proposed bill to his priority agenda. Congresswoman Sullivan fought strong lobbyists for business firms on issues of special treatment for loan sharks and the American Retail Federation on the secrecy practiced in regard to revolving credit plans.

Her dedication and integrity won the respect and votes needed to pass HR 11601. The final comprehensive Consumer Credit Protection Act of 1968 (known as truth-in-lending) was signed by President Lyndon B. Johnson with the following special tribute to Mrs. Sullivan: "This bill was made possible by that able congresswoman from Missouri who fought, and I say fought . . . for a strong and effective bill when others would have settled for less." In 1970, she introduced in the House and helped to pass a "Fair Credit Reporting Act" that would enable consumers to protect themselves against arbitrary, erroneous, and malicious information sold by credit reporting companies to users of their services. Congresswoman Sullivan says smilingly, "The passage of that legislation gave me one of the greatest joys and sense of satisfaction as a congresswoman."

Another personal success began in 1954 with the introduction of the first food stamp law which Congresswoman Sullivan authored. Concern for the millions of poor people in our country caused her to seek ways to better their lives. She proposed distribution of surplus commodities to the needy through local grocery stores through the use of food stamps. However, the law was not implemented by President Eisenhower. A modified pilot food stamp plan was lauched by President Kennedy, and this led to Congresswoman Sullivan's introduction in the 88th Congress of an administration food stamp bill that was enacted into law on August 11, 1964.

When asked what areas appear to need the skills and talents of congresswomen most, Mrs. Sullivan replied ". . . I believe that congresswomen are needed in areas that relate to the family and consumer matters," she began. "Personally, I'm convinced women can make the most impact in Congress by remaining feminine. And, of course, they must do their homework—be informed. I also believe that the minds of men and women work and react differently. And this is good. Because as long as women continue in this manner and bring their feminine thoughts and reactions into the legislative discussions, a good compromise can be made along with the male thinking and reactions." Her solemn intonation left no doubt of her sincerity and convictions with this listener.

Her interest in matters of family are demonstrated by the leading role she played in the preparation of all housing bills passed by the House since 1955. Congresswoman Sullivan opposed high rise public housing for families with children, stressing the desirability of low garden-type buildings that might promote family cohesiveness and stability. Mrs. Sullivan supported regulations which would require public housing tenants to assume more responsibility for the maintenance and supervision of their housing units. Housing for the elderly and programs enabling low-income families to purchase rehabilitated homes received her endorsement, too. She was an advocate of safe foods, drugs, and cosmetics. During the 91st Congress, the congresswoman was chairman of an ad hoc subcommittee which investigated alleged irregularities of lending institutions which issued federally insured real estate loans in inner-city communities.

In 1957, Congresswoman Sullivan drafted and introduced legislation entitled, The Exceptional Children Educational Assistance Bill—the first ever submitted to the House. Its purpose was to encourage experienced teachers to take advanced training in the skills of teaching gifted children or those with physical or emotional handicaps. Subsequently, fellowship programs were established for teachers of all categories of handicapped children.

It is not difficult to understand Mrs. Sullivan's passion for the poor and for the family unit. Born Leonor Alice Kretzer, she was one in a family of nine children. Her father worked as a partner in his father's custom tailoring business to provide for the large Catholic family. He was a believer in the American system which considers everything and anything possible if one perseveres. Unable to finance a college education, she started her business career as a $35.00 a-month telephone company clerk. Later, Congresswoman Sullivan advanced from a demonstrator of office machines to a training executive in a St. Louis business firm. At times, she was responsible for the education of as many as 2000 trainees a year. This experience of working with all kinds of people contributed to her later success as a congresswoman. But like many young women, she looked forward to marriage and family. In 1941, she became Mrs. John Berchmans Sullivan. Her new husband was serving his first term as a member of the United States House of Representatives. The next four years she worked beside him as an unpaid aide. She learned quickly and easily and later was a paid assistant. It was during these years that she grew to realize the contributions and service that were possible by an honest, dedicated, and capable public servant.

Many people, both men and women, feel the roles of wife, mother, and politician are full of conflict. Congresswoman Sullivan expressed her feelings like this. "Since I had no children, I was not faced with the necessity of adapting to the roles of mother and politician. However, from my observations, it would seem to be most difficult to combine the three careers successfully—(that of wife, mother, and a member of Congress)—until the children are of an age where their characters have been guided and formed by a proper home atmosphere." She paused in a reflective mood. "I believe that a matured woman who has had the experience of raising children along with a cooperative husband has much to offer in public service. But it is so much easier after these responsibilities have been met." Congresswoman Sullivan believes that women are emotionally suitable for political leadership, but she strongly believes also that a woman's most important role, if she marries, is in the home. "Wholesome family life is the mainstay of our civilization," she contends. Her uncertainty that the legal effects of the Equal Rights Amendment (ERA) could contribute to the dissolution of family life caused her to vote against it in the 92nd Congress. She stood alone bravely to cast the only negative vote by a congresswoman.

Congresswoman Sullivan can recall some unpleasant and

disappointing moments in her long career too. "I think the greatest disaster or disappointment of a legislative body is poor administration of some of the laws we have passed . . . especially some that I personally sponsored. Look at the Food Stamp Act, for example. There were others like housing for low-income people and the bungling of our welfare assistance programs."

To the question of getting congressmen to take her seriously, she replies. "Well . . . frankly I faced no problem in having them take me seriously. I believe they recognized my sincerity, and also I was not in the habit of speaking on *every* subject. When I did speak, I had done as much research possible so they knew I was serious in my support or opposition to any given subject or issue."

Although it is twenty-four years since Mrs. Sullivan came to Congress, she doesn't see much change or movement toward equalization of the sexes. She remarks, "A woman can be treated as an equal, if her knowledge and her ability, along with her conduct, entitle her to that equality. Many women have been appreciated and recognized for the contribution they have made while serving as members of Congress."

Mrs. Sullivan advises young women on preparation for public service careers in this way. "I think the best way is to become interested in legislation and the affairs of the local community—especially in the types of problems that touch the lives of the people. She should also become active in the political party of her choice. It is vital that she become known in the community before offering herself for election to public office. And most important, she must be willing to become a public servant. In my newsletter, *Speaking From Washington,* I encouraged my constituents to communicate their problems to me so that I could be helpful."

There is no question about Congresswoman Sullivan being a public servant. She loved her work and derived tremendous satisfaction from the arduous tasks that occupied fourteen to sixteen hours of her day for almost two dozen years. Her list of accomplishments is endless and impressive. Most work in Congress is accomplished through committees, and the following committees have gained from her contributions as a member:

National Commission on Food Marketing, 1964-66

National Commission on Mortgage Interest Rates, 1968-69

National Commission on Consumer Finance, 1969-72

U.S. Territorial Expansion Memorial Commission (chairman)

House Committee on Merchant Marine and Fisheries, 83rd-94th Congresses: chairman, 93rd-94th Congresses; chairman, Subcommittee on Panama Canal, 85th-91st Congresses

House Committee on Banking and Currency (now Banking, Currency and Housing), 84th-94th Congresses: chairman, Subcommittee on Consumer Affairs, 88th-93rd Congresses; chairman, Special Subcommittee Investigating Home Financing Practices and Abuses, 91st Congress; member, Subcommittee on Housing, 84th-94th Congresses

Joint Committee on Defense Production, 90th-94th Congresses

After reading her long list of credits, one wonders where she got so much energy. "Only the Lord knows that! I've been fortunate enough to have good health. I am an enthusiastic person. I love people! I loved my work. And I feel this combination has reinforced my efforts and helped to give me the energy and strength to meet the heavy demands on my time," the congresswoman concludes.

One of the highlights of Congresswoman Sullivan's career

was the impressive ceremony for the unveiling of her portrait held on September 24, 1974. This is a great honor, and is not bestowed lightly. The beautiful oil painting by the well-known artist, Charles J. Fox, is mounted behind the dais in the Merchant Marine and Fisheries Committee hearing room in the Longworth House Office Building. In the portrait, she is shown wearing an off-white knit dress against a background of muted pastel colors. Honesty and sincerity are reflected in her soft, blue-green eyes. The half-smile soften a face which is attractive and yet full of character. Strength of purpose and determination are communicated to the viewer through her regal posture. Her long-time friend, President Gerald Ford, honored her with these remarks: "There have been no other members who I think enjoy the respect and admiration, Democratic or Republican, more than you; but most of all, I am proud to call you a friend and to wish you the very best."

With all of these wonderful memories, it was most difficult for Congresswoman Sullivan to say goodbye to her colleagues and many friends on Capitol Hill in January 1977. But dedication to millions of constituents and to so many causes for so many years takes its toll. Mrs. Sullivan is no part-time congresswoman! She leaves behind many unfinished tasks that she initiated, but her dominant spirit remains as a heritage to spur others to the challenge.

Many people feel that women do not participate fully in the democratic process. The congresswoman speaks out forcefully. "I believe women are participating to the extent that they *desire* and are *willing* to make the sacrifices necessary for that participation." For those who might follow this dynamic, conservative path-blazer, she has made the job easier because of her example of total devotion to duty and service to her constituency and to the nation.

The congresswoman has some final words for young

women. "If a young woman wants a career in public service, then she must prepare herself. Be honest and frank in presenting her real desire to serve," Congresswoman Sullivan counsels.

With such a long and full career behind her, one wonders if she would do things differently if she had the chance to relive her life. She ponders the question for a moment. "Well . . . probably I would have taken the time out to romance and possibly fall in love again." Her expression becomes pensive and somewhat wistful, but she continues. "You see . . . it was my husband's example of dedication to our government that induced me to follow his career after his death. As a business woman, I was greatly in love with the work I performed and therefore it was very hard for me back there in 1941 to make that big decision. I had to make up my mind to give up a good job I loved and had spent so much time developing and marry and become dependent upon a man." Congresswoman Sullivan chuckles softly. "It's something that I have thought about so often. I've always felt that when you marry, you enter a career. And of course, my career hopefully would be raising a family and having a good husband . . . sort of living or reliving the life that I knew as a child with wonderful parents and a happy family life."

Fortunately for all of us, John Sullivan convinced Leonor Sullivan that a political life could be a good one. Politics is only bad when the wrong people get elected. His inspiration changed a shy, self-conscious, young woman into a legend. Congresswoman Sullivan's act will be hard to follow, but she's demonstrated that not only can women perform but they can become stars in a male dominated arena. She will have time now to experience the unfamiliar joy of learning how to loaf, a luxury she has not known since she was a young teenager.

Index